INCLUDING ALL CHILDREN

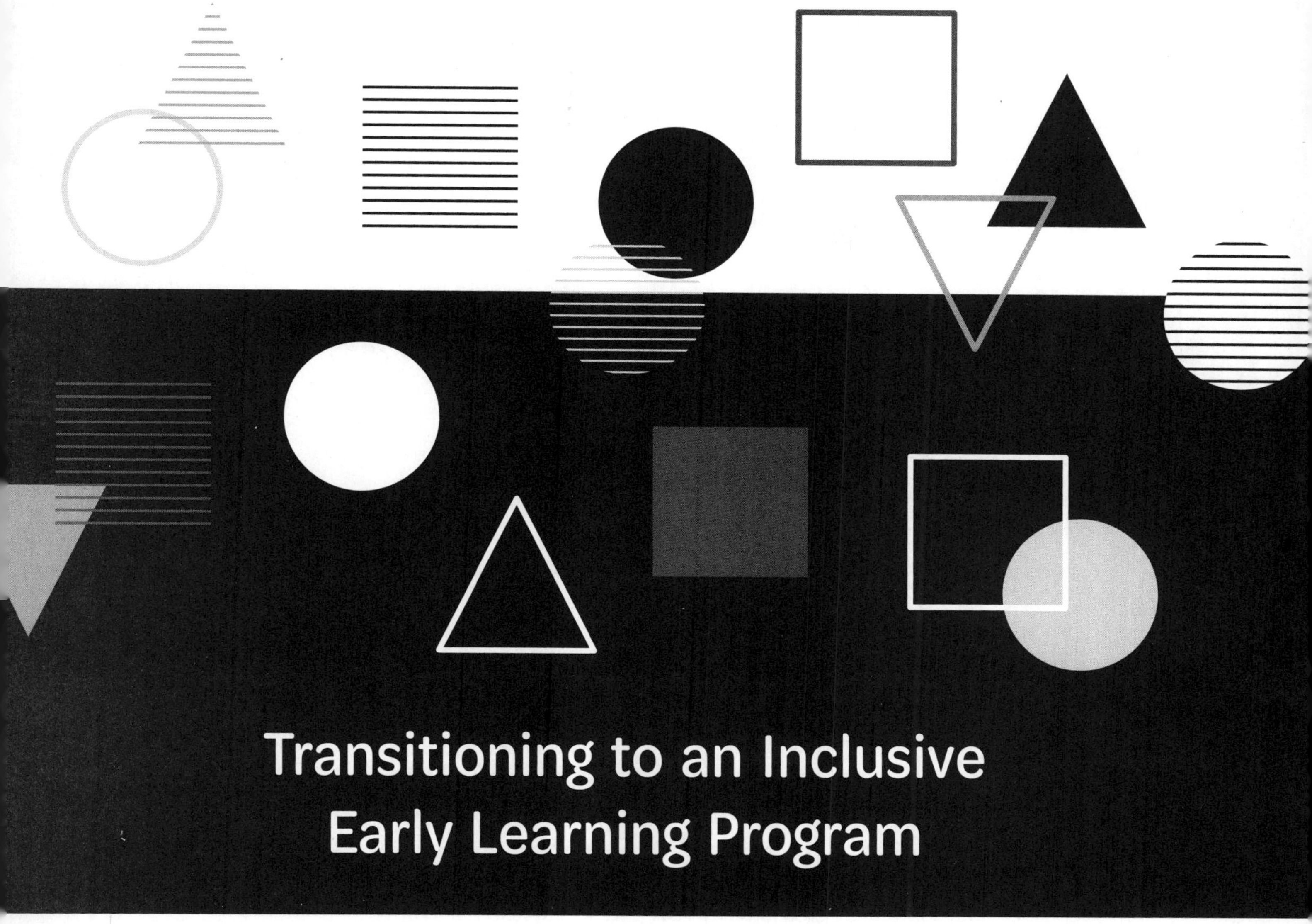

Transitioning to an Inclusive Early Learning Program

Sarah Taylor Vanover, EdD

Copyright

© 2023 Sarah Taylor Vanover

Published by GRYPHON House, Inc.
P. O. Box 10, Lewisville, NC 27023
800.638.0928; 877.638.7576 [fax]

Visit us on the web at www.gryphonhouse.com.

All rights reserved. No part of this publication may be reproduced or transmitted in any form or by any means, electronic or technical, including photocopy, recording, or any information storage or retrieval system, without prior written permission of the publisher. Printed in the United States. Every effort has been made to locate copyright and permission information.

Cover images used under license from Shutterstock.com and courtesy of the author.

Library of Congress Control Number: 2023932096

Bulk Purchase

Gryphon House books are available for special premiums and sales promotions as well as for fund-raising use. Special editions or book excerpts also can be created to specifications. For details, call 800.638.0928.

Disclaimer

Gryphon House, Inc., cannot be held responsible for damage, mishap, or injury incurred during the use of or because of activities in this book. Appropriate and reasonable caution and adult supervision of children involved in activities and corresponding to the age and capability of each child involved are recommended at all times. Do not leave children unattended at any time. Observe safety and caution at all times. This book is not intended to give legal or financial advice. All financial and legal opinions contained herein are from the personal research and experience of the author and are intended as educational material. Seek the advice of a qualified legal advisor or financial advisor before making legal or financial decisions.

DEDICATION

This book is dedicated to Rebecca Hill, Marissa Cupp, Jasmine Jones, Dr. Jeremy Warner, Dr. Susan Slade, and all the amazing professionals who have been a member of my son's support team. I am so thankful for each pediatric expert who has supported him so that he can be successful in an inclusive classroom.

TABLE OF CONTENTS

PREFACE: My Story v

CHAPTER 1: Defining Inclusion 1

CHAPTER 2: Laws Surrounding Special Education 27

CHAPTER 3: Vision and Mission Statements 35

CHAPTER 4: Starting the Transition 52

CHAPTER 5: Setting New Policies 57

CHAPTER 6: Creating Accommodations 76

CHAPTER 7: Supporting Teaching Staff
in the Inclusive Classroom 90

CHAPTER 8: Collaboration and Inclusion 107

APPENDIX: Child-Care Self-Evaluation for Inclusive Programs ... 117

REFERENCES AND RECOMMENDED READING 127

INDEX 130

PREFACE: MY STORY

When I was a child, I knew what disabilities were, but they were so far removed from my world that they seemed unrealistic. My family was healthy, and we seemed to lead a relatively normal life. Unfortunately, that track record ended in high school.

At the beginning of my sophomore year, I began having fainting spells. The pediatrician attributed them to low blood sugar and told me that I needed to have four to six small meals throughout the day to keep my blood sugar levels higher and more consistent. Then one day in choir, I stood up to join a small group of singers in the hallway and fainted, falling down the choir risers. I woke up confused while EMTs secured me to a gurney and took me to the emergency room. There, the doctor thought that it was time I see a specialist, and she connected my parents with a pediatric endocrinologist at a large hospital two hours away from my hometown. We spent a week in the hospital, and at the end of our visit, the doctor determined that severe drops in my blood sugar were causing me to lose consciousness. The doctor put me on a diabetic diet, told me to check my blood sugar three to five times a day, and scheduled follow-up visits every two months.

I tried to eat what I was supposed to eat, but I was fifteen years old and didn't understand the full impact of ignoring a doctor's orders. There were times that I indulged in milkshakes and candy bars, but that usually came with consequences. Eating something with lots of sugar would rebound and make my blood sugar crash again. When I became dizzy or passed out, I would promise that I wouldn't ignore my diet again. Of course, there were always mistakes, but they happened less often as the months went on and I battled against my sweet tooth.

I was an active teenager, and I always had places to be. I was really involved in my school choir and at my church. In the spring of my junior year of high school, I arrived at church early one Sunday so that I could prepare to lead worship in our church service. While singing in the service that morning, I had a grand mal seizure in front of the entire congregation. Although sixteen-year-old girls tend to thrive on attention, this was not the type of attention I wanted. I woke up in the ambulance on the way to the hospital and had no memory of what had occurred at church. Tests showed that there was enough electrical activity to indicate that I did indeed have a seizure. The doctor told me that one seizure did not mean that I had a seizure disorder, but it did mean that the doctor needed to watch me closely. It also meant that I could not drive for the next ninety days due to state law.

Three months later, I was at a summer music camp in Santa Barbara, California, and I had a second grand mal seizure. Once again, I did not remember anything that had happened, but this time I was a long way from home. My parents had been so apprehensive about letting me go to camp after the first seizure occurred, but I had begged them to let me go because my health had been fine. The day after the seizure, I flew home to Kentucky, and my mom was already working on finding a pediatric neurologist who could help us understand what was going on. This time I ended up at Washington University Hospital in St. Louis, Missouri, where, after a long week of lots of tests, the pediatric neurologist diagnosed epilepsy.

Before we left, the doctor started me on the first of many anti-convulsant medications I would take in my lifetime. Throughout my senior year and most of college, I struggled with remembering to take my medication, avoiding caffeine, and getting enough sleep. Stress was also a major trigger for my seizures. In college, you could almost track my seizures around midterms and finals, when I was stressed and sleep deprived. Each time it happened, I lost my driver's license. As a young adult, that was the part that upset me the most. Of course, I had friends who would take me places when I needed them to, but the loss of my independence was the frustrating part. My illness also came with many doctor visits and a lot of medication side effects. During the first four years of my diagnosis, I must have tried at least five different seizure medications. It took a long time to find the right medication, and then the doctor had to find the right dosage.

While I was worried about my medication, my parents were trying to find a way to cover the cost of the doctor visits, the tests, the MRIs, and the medication. We were blessed to have good health insurance, but it didn't cover all the expenses that I was collecting. My mom became an expert at fighting with health insurance companies. Before I went to college, we took one trip to campus just to find a neurologist who was close enough for me to visit for regular medical care. We looked for a pharmacy where I could get my medication. My father switched jobs while I was in college, and we had to prove that I did not have a breach in medical coverage to keep getting treatment for my pre-existing condition. When you looked at me, you couldn't notice anything visibly wrong, but my diagnosis was starting to be a huge part of my life.

I have spent a large portion of my life trying to live as if I don't have a disability. I pursued higher education through my doctorate degree, regardless of the stress and hours of study that it included. I had two healthy children, even though I was a high-risk pregnancy each time, which required quite a few extra doctor appointments. Many times, I have taken on too much work and responsibility, and I wonder sometimes if I am just trying to prove that I can do anything that a "normal" person can do. In the end, a high stress load always comes back to haunt me. The only way to really live with, and even overcome, my disability is to take care of myself and admit when something is just too much for me.

While I was in college, I decided that I wanted to major in early childhood education. I had always wanted to do something with young children. At first, I think I was a little more interested in what it "looked like" to be a preschool teacher. I loved their colorful classrooms with the alphabet and shapes displayed on the walls. I loved watching teachers read dramatic stories to the children and sing silly songs while the children danced around on the carpet. It seemed like an inconvenience when the teacher had to spend time dealing with the children's negative behaviors, but because I was observing veteran teachers, they always seemed to handle the situation so effortlessly.

As I got closer to graduating and pursuing my teacher's certificate, I began thinking about the type of classroom in which I wanted to work. In early childhood education, I could go into a traditional play-based preschool classroom or a classroom that also supported children with special needs. At that point in my career, those two options seemed completely separate: a "normal" classroom or a classroom that had children with disabilities. It seemed more fun to get a job in a traditional preschool classroom where I could do curriculum units on farm animals and community helpers. I would be able to have all the children in my classroom sit at circle time at once and read *Harry, the Dirty Dog* or *The Very Hungry Caterpillar* to them. I envisioned all the children being able to do the same activities and participate together.

My first teaching job was in a private school that served children in the three-year-old preschool through sixth grade. It was a beautiful campus filled with well-organized classrooms and teachers who had worked with young children for years. I was in a blended classroom that had three-, four-, and five-year-old students, and I had two co-teachers.

The week before the school year started, at open house, I met Jacob and his family. Jacob was an incoming three-year-old child. His mother and father both attended the open house, but his father was preparing to leave the country for the next three weeks. The family was in the middle of an international adoption, and Mr. Ralph was going to travel to Asia to pick up their newborn baby girl while Mrs. Ralph stayed at home with Jacob.

The new school year started, and Jacob arrived on the first day wearing a backpack that was almost bigger than his whole body. Just like several of the other three-year-olds, he was apprehensive of his new surroundings and scared to leave his mother. On the first day, Jacob had two bathroom accidents that were very messy. I cleaned him up and put clean clothes on him. I communicated with his mother to let her know what had happened. My co-teacher, who had taught at the school for twelve years, told Mrs. Ralph that it wasn't unusual for children to have accidents on the first couple of days of school

because they are so interested in the new classroom that they don't want to take the time to stop playing and go use the restroom. Mrs. Ralph seemed fine with the situation and took the setback in stride. Unfortunately, Jacob's accidents didn't just happen for a few days; they became a consistent pattern. Because I was the primary caregiver for the three-year-olds, I grew accustomed to helping Jacob clean up and continue with his school day. I had worked in a child-care program before being hired at this new school, so I was familiar with helping students through the potty-training process.

A couple of weeks later, Jacob had another accident, but I had left the room. One of my co-teachers had to help Jacob clean up, and it was apparent at that point that my co-teachers had a very different idea of what was appropriate for a preschool classroom compared to my interpretation. That afternoon, my co-teachers asked Mrs. Ralph to come in for a conference. Mr. Ralph was still in Asia, and he would not return for four more days. With the support of the school principal, my co-teachers told Mrs. Ralph that Jacob was not developmentally ready to start preschool. They suggested that she find a different child-care program and possibly apply again next year for our school. At that moment, Mrs. Ralph was alone as she received the overwhelming news. She worked outside of the home, but she no longer had child care. The school did not acknowledge the potential trauma that Jacob may have been experiencing while his father was away or as he processed the knowledge that he had a baby sister coming. No accommodations were made. They simply told the family that Jacob was not a good fit for the school.

As I sat back and watched this situation evolve, I was overwhelmed by the whole situation. This was my first teaching position after receiving my teacher's certificate, and I didn't know if this was a typical situation. I thought I was in a "normal" classroom, so it seemed odd that a child was not toilet trained at three years old. But I had previously worked with four-year-old children with whom the problem didn't really come up. I convinced myself that the situation was a fluke and tried to go back to my "typical" school year.

Later that year I started to notice some strange behaviors from one of the other three-year-old children in my group. Everett was one of my youngest students, and he was smaller than any other child in the classroom. He seemed like he walked around the classroom in a fog most of the time. When he tried to pick up the classroom materials, it was a challenge for him to carry them to a table because he was so small. Often when Everett was walking around the room, he would slow to a stop and just stare off into space. I would have to call out his name and get his attention to redirect him. He had also begun to wet his pants at least once a day. This was odd because he had been completely toilet trained with no accidents and then seemed to suddenly regress. My child-development background had taught me that you could not diagnose children with attention-deficit disorder until they are much older than three, but it seemed that he was constantly distracted.

As I spent more time with Everett, I began to realize that he did not realize that he was staring off into space. When I was finally able to get his attention, he often seemed to have forgotten where he was. I noticed this same type of behavior when he had a bathroom accident. I was the one who told him that his pants were wet, and he had no recollection of why he had not gone to the restroom. With my own personal history of epilepsy, these symptoms sounded familiar to me. I talked to my co-teachers and discussed calling the parents to let them know the symptoms we were seeing in the classroom: blank stares, confusion, incontinence, and small losses of time. We recommended that the family take Everett to his pediatrician to discuss his symptoms. Two months later, Everett was at the neurologist getting evaluated for absence seizures. When my co-teachers learned about Everett's diagnosis, they were instantly uncomfortable with caring for a child with special health-care needs. I did not have any medical training, but I had been learning for years about how to support someone with epilepsy. I immediately let the principal know that I felt completely comfortable caring for Everett, and I just needed a conference with his parents to see how his doctor planned to treat his condition. My principal agreed.

This preschool program was supposed to serve "typical" students. They interviewed each family in advance and admitted the children who seemed the most capable to thrive in a structured preschool program. Despite the school's efforts, there were still children in the program who needed accommodations and additional support. I noticed very quickly that the school was not set up to offer that support, and because of that, students like Jacob were told to find a program that could better meet their needs. The whole family was affected when the school could not support a child enrolled in the program. I also realized that it wasn't the children who needed to change; it was the school. The teachers needed more training on how to work with children with disabilities or special health-care needs. The classroom materials needed to accommodate a wider range of skills so that children of different ability levels could play.

After two years of teaching at the private preschool, my interests had changed. I applied for a position with a local school system as an early childhood special-education teacher. I wanted to work with the children my previous school could not support. I accepted a preschool teacher position for a classroom of students with disabilities and students who were considered "at risk" due to living at the poverty level. By the second week of school, I had seventeen children in my classroom, and sixteen of those children were diagnosed with disabilities.

My assistant teacher and I were completely overwhelmed. Several of the children in our classroom had significant disabilities, such as autism, cerebral palsy, fetal alcohol syndrome, and cognitive delays. The other students in the classroom had milder conditions but still suffered from some type of delay. There were no typically developing children in the classroom to serve as role models, and the children in our room seemed separated from the rest of the school. Although I was supporting the children whom I wanted to help, I was overwhelmed and didn't feel like I was accomplishing anything. The students needed so much more support than I felt I could offer, and it didn't seem as though I could spend enough individual time with each child.

In short, this classroom setting didn't seem to be right either. Students with disabilities needed a preschool setting that gave them proper support, but totally isolating them made the workload overwhelming for the teachers and didn't give the children enough room to grow. The K–12 education system already had made great strides in setting up inclusive classrooms and placing children in the least restrictive environment (LRE). They had moved away from isolating children in special-education classrooms and were allowing them to stay in the typical classroom setting as much as possible. It baffled me that the birth-to-five education system seemed to be miles behind.

The root of this problem is that most children between the ages of infancy and kindergarten are eligible to be cared for in private child-care programs that are independent small businesses. Unlike the K–12 school system, they do not receive special-education funding to pay for additional staff members, training, and modified materials that children with disabilities may need. Children qualify for the public school system when they have a diagnosed disability, so many of those children naturally find a special-education preschool classroom. What needs to happen for the early education community is to find a way to blend these two environments to care for all types of children in inclusive classrooms.

Fast forward nine years, when I was pregnant with my second child, I felt like I had a soccer player inside my belly. He moved and kicked every few minutes, day or night. When he was finally born, he did not calm down. He was diagnosed with colic by the time he was five weeks old, and he spent more than two-thirds of his waking hours screaming at the top of his lungs. He was feisty from the beginning.

With his great desire to move, he was up and moving every single night. He didn't sleep through the night for the first time until he turned thirteen months old. He became very attached to me and wouldn't let anyone else feed him. In fact, he wouldn't drink from a bottle at all; he would only breastfeed. When we tried to introduce baby food and eventually table food, it was a struggle. Luckily, I was working as the executive director of a private, nonprofit, inclusive child-care program at the time, and the amazing occupational therapist on staff was giving me tips to help ease him through this transition.

Because he was always on the move, he crawled and walked ahead of developmental norms. My husband sang to him every night, and I read him books. We were constantly talking to him and his big brother, even when he couldn't respond to us yet. Because of hearing so much language at a young age, he was an early talker, and by age two he had a huge vocabulary. You could tell that he was smart because of his vocabulary and because he was a problem-solver. He would work through frustrations with his toys on his own and never let difficulties slow him down. Not only was he smart, but he was also stubborn.

I don't want to make stubborn sound like a bad thing. My son had an iron will at a very young age. When he made up his mind to do something, he was determined and steadfast. This determination could be positive or negative. He could be determined to complete a puzzle or he could be determined not to eat his dinner. He would refuse to speak to people that he did not know, and even if they tried to wear him down, he would not speak to them. When my son switched to his first preschool classroom, we enrolled him in a private, employee-based child-care program. After he initially started at the school, it took him almost three months before he would speak to the teacher. When he finally did talk to her, she was ecstatic! Sometimes, a teacher who did not know him might try to make him do something such as eat all of his lunch or go to sleep at naptime. That was like someone throwing down a gauntlet, and James was going to rise to the occasion. Nothing was more important to him than being right or doing something the right way (as he saw it).

He was content to play at school. He loved to play with dress-up clothes, color pictures, and do puzzles, but he often did these activities alone. He was a reserved child and did not like to be around the noisy, outgoing children. He would find a quieter place in the classroom and play contentedly, usually beside another quiet child. Because he went to a high-quality preschool program, the school gave him some flexibility. If it was too overwhelming for him to sit at circle time with the other children, then the teachers let him quietly play in the back of the classroom. He usually heard all of the songs and the calendar, but he didn't have to be overwhelmed by the large group of children. Instead of forcing him to do one particular activity, the teachers tried to give him choices so that he felt more in control. Also, he had wise teachers who decided to pick their battles and only insist on his compliance when it came to a safety issue.

When my son started kindergarten at our public elementary school, I began to see him struggle in different ways. The school day was structured and fast-paced. If the whole classroom needed to move on to the next activity before he finished his work, then he would be overwhelmed by the transition. Activities such as circle time were hard for him to participate in, and they caused him to panic. Usually that panic led to a fight-or-flight reaction. At school, he would usually hide under a desk or in the corner of the classroom when he was overwhelmed by the pace of the day or was scared by not knowing what was coming next. At home, where he was most comfortable, that panic would often result in yelling and hitting. He did not want any type of social attention, so activities such as morning greetings could cause him anxiety hours before he arrived at school. Fun days, like Crazy Sock Day, meant that children would be staring at him all day to see what socks he had on, and that also caused stress.

The kindergarten teacher called me on the first day of school and asked me about strategies that we use at home to help him be successful. It's never a good sign when the teacher calls you on the first day. My husband kept asking me, "Should we be worried yet?" I was telling him that our child was smart, stubborn, and shy. We just needed to watch him grow and see if he moved through some of these phases. During this period I started to notice that, although his vocabulary was huge, he didn't always use his speech in the socially correct way. Other children his age were starting to make jokes that easily offended him. He would say things that seemed extremely rude, but he seemed to think he was being helpful. He seemed to insult me frequently, and as a mom, that was hard to take. I asked the school for a speech evaluation to look at the way that he used his vocabulary because it just seemed off. The school said he passed his speech evaluation with flying colors, and he graduated from kindergarten with a lot of unanswered questions.

The next year in first grade was much more challenging. The emotional meltdowns were occurring all the time. At home they became violent, but at school, he hid and couldn't regroup for the remainder of the school day. As he became more and more aggressive with me and my older son, I told my husband that it was time to get help. I thought maybe he was showing signs of oppositional defiant disorder, since he was so stubborn and rigid. Once we finally found a counselor who was willing to see a six-year-old, she felt she was seeing signs of significant anxiety and possible autism spectrum disorder. Looking back, that is the point that I had to become an advocate for my child. I started an uphill battle that day.

I began looking for specialists who could evaluate my child for autism. I called universities and private physician practices. Before they could agree to make an appointment, I needed to fill out dozens of forms and screening tools to see if he qualified for an evaluation. Once I had taken off the rose-colored glasses of being his mother and tried to see him from the viewpoint of a professional, I realized that he had a lot of the criteria that the diagnosticians were looking for before consenting to an evaluation. I was calling so many specialists to try and get him on at least one waiting list, and they all had different forms. I decided to make one log of all the symptoms and concerns that I had noticed since he was an infant. I kept a running Word document that I added to over time, and I printed it off for each new doctor that we met with.

As someone with a background in special education, I was lucky that I knew a lot of therapists and specialists in the field. I had never asked for favors from anyone before, but now I was trying to help my son and would do anything I could to support him. I had reached out to a pediatric occupational therapist whom I had worked with before to ask her to start seeing my son. She said that it would be six months before she would have an opening in her schedule, but she was willing to call a child psychiatrist she knew to ask her to fit my son into her busy schedule. Then, I had to find an occupational therapist to see him, and after all the money I had spent on autism evaluations, second opinions, and psychiatric evaluations, I had to find a practice that would take my health insurance.

When I talked to my pediatrician about my son, he still couldn't believe the autism diagnosis. My son didn't fit the textbook case of a nonverbal boy who was obsessed with trains. Instead, he was a seven-year-old with an IQ of 140 who had a challenging time dealing with transitions and changes to routines. I would tell people close to me that he was diagnosed with autism, and they would say, "He doesn't look like he has autism." Even when a close friend or family member would say something so foolish, I wanted to respond by saying something like, "Well, we parted his hair on the left today, so that's why you can't tell."

My fight for my son started by getting his diagnosis and the best medical care possible, but my fight continues when it comes to getting him the best possible education. Because he has a high IQ, the school doesn't always agree that his disability is affecting his schoolwork, which is the whole purpose of special education. Instead, I must prove to the school system every year that his emotional meltdowns at school and his intense anxiety limit his ability to be successful. I have to show them that he needs accommodations such as movement breaks during the day and advance notification of changes to his school routine.

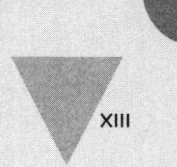

Being the parent of a child with a disability is challenging. Daily, I may have to fight the health insurance company, the school system, and the director of the local gymnastics classes just to let him have normal childhood experiences. I have started this battle with resources that many families don't have and with a strong knowledge of the special-education system. I just don't understand how families can navigate this situation if they don't know who to turn to and what their child needs. Every family deserves the right to help their children be successful.

■ ■ ■

My experiences have shaped me as an individual with a disability, as a teacher, and as a mother. My perspective on special education has been created by all three points of view. As an adult living with a disability (epilepsy), I understand how hard it may be to overcome stereotypes, take care of yourself properly, and live in a world where others don't understand your limitations. As an early childhood teacher, I've seen children who desperately needed a classroom and an education system that would support them no matter what their ability level was. As a parent of a child with autism, I learned a deep empathy for children with disabilities and their families, empathy that I did not understand as a young teacher or an administrator. I now have a passion for inclusive early childhood education, which is the driving force in my career and what propelled me to write this book.

CHAPTER 1

Defining Inclusion

The need for inclusive child care in the United States is overwhelming. The US Census Bureau indicates that more than three million children had a diagnosed disability in 2019, which was approximately 4.3 percent of the total child population. The Centers for Disease Control and Prevention (CDC) and the Health Resources Services Administration (HRSA) state that 17 percent of children between the ages of three and seventeen have a developmental delay and need assistance to catch up to the normal developmental milestones (2022). This means that one in six children needs additional educational support to be successful (Young and Crankshaw, 2021). The CDC and HRSA (2022) also found that the following groups were more likely to have a developmental delay than others:

- Boys had a greater chance of a delay than girls.

- Non-Hispanic children (both Black and White) were more likely to have a diagnosed delay than Hispanic children.

- Children in rural areas had a greater chance of a diagnosis compared to children living in urban areas.

- Children on public health insurance were more likely to have a developmental delay than children on private health insurance or children who are uninsured.

There is a difference between a disability and a developmental delay. *Developmental delay* is a term used when a child is behind the typical timeline for meeting developmental milestones. If a young child receives therapeutic support for a developmental delay in a timely fashion, then the child may not have a permanent developmental delay. Most schools will try to use the term *developmental delay* until the child turns eight years of age to see if the diagnosis is temporary. The term *disability* is a more permanent diagnosis. It is typically related to a medical diagnosis that affects a child's mental and physical development.

Early intervention and inclusive preschool services have been accessible throughout the United States for years; however, the COVID-19 pandemic affected many children's ability to access those services (Shapiro and Bassok, 2022). Early education classrooms had to suspend in-person classroom time. The core principles of child development are focused on children learning by exploring the environment through their senses. When young children are limited to watching a screen for learning, many of those key learning skills are limited (Shapiro and Bassok, 2022).

Many families dropped out of virtual preschool programs because they saw their children's lack of interest. Plus, one of the foundational skills of preschool is social and emotional learning with a group of peers, and peer interaction was not possible on a computer screen. Children could see their peers and talk to them, but they could not learn to share or engage in group play. Once classrooms resumed in-person learning, it was obvious that many children were not at the developmental level that is typically expected in their age range. With early interventions, most toddlers and young preschoolers could not show more than a few minutes of interest in a computer screen, much less complete an activity with the therapist. Therefore, children who were already diagnosed with a developmental delay or a disability prior to the pandemic rarely made developmental strides during this period, and most saw developmental losses (Shapiro and Bassok, 2022).

As a society, our goal should be to establish a seamless education system that supports **all** children, beginning in the infant room. We cannot wait until a child starts kindergarten to provide an inclusive environment. Many child-care programs do not know what they need to do to support more families of children with disabilities. They do not understand what policies need to be in place to accommodate children with disabilities or special health-care needs. This book is a guide to help early childhood educators care for all children, regardless of ability level, by creating an inclusive child-care program.

ABOUT THIS BOOK

If you are reading this book, you're probably interested in creating an inclusive learning environment but are unsure of how to go about it. Perhaps you're not sure if your teaching staff and the families you serve understand why offering an inclusive program is important. Perhaps you are concerned about the changes you'll need to make to your classroom environment, materials, and curriculum. Or perhaps you are just beginning to delve into inclusive child-care programs and want to have a sense of where to begin. This book will help you answer your questions, alleviate your concerns, remove roadblocks, and get you on your way.

This first chapter provides an introductory discussion about inclusive child-care programs: what it means to be inclusive and why it is beneficial. Chapter 2 describes the different laws surrounding special education. Building on this background, chapter 3 delves into the first step in creating an inclusive child-care program: drafting a vision and mission statement to reflect your program's approach. Chapter 4 provides an overview of how you might start the transition, and chapters 5 and 6 get into the nitty-gritty of becoming an inclusive child-care program: setting policies and creating accommodations to support children with disabilities and their families. The final two chapters of this book discuss supporting staff in the inclusive classroom and collaborating with families and the community.

Interspersed throughout the chapters are personal perspectives from a parent of a child with disabilities, an early childhood director, a child-care provider, and a pediatric occupational therapist. These personal perspectives are included to show real-life examples of what families and professionals see when they enter inclusive and noninclusive classrooms. Their examples show how the inclusive environment benefits all the enrolled children in the classroom, not just those identified with developmental delays. They also show how the family and the teachers can have positive experiences by looking at a more individualized approach to education.

The first story shows the perspective of a family who desperately needed an inclusive child-care setting for their foster children. The children were turned away from other programs, and they needed the support that only an inclusive program could offer. The second story is from the perspective of a director who administers an inclusive child-care program. She has had the opportunity to see so many successes for children struggling with their delays, and she has gotten to watch those children grow and develop over time with supportive services. An early interventionist gives her perspective on inclusive child care after going into hundreds of child-care classrooms in her career, and a veteran early childhood educator who has worked in both inclusive and noninclusive programs shares her experiences with the program administration and with the children.

WHAT DOES AN INCLUSIVE EARLY CLASSROOM LOOK LIKE?

In 2009, two of the largest early childhood organizations collaborated to write a joint position statement on what an inclusive early childhood classroom should look like. According to the Division of Early Childhood and the National Association for the Education of Young Children (2009), inclusive early childhood environments have several different characteristics:

- Every infant and young child should be able to practice in a variety of learning activities, regardless of the child's ability level.

- Children will have access to classroom activities and environments by removing physical barriers and providing a variety of learning activities.

- Classrooms will encourage participation for all children by using play-based learning and implementing a variety of learning strategies to help all children be a part of the learning community.

- Teachers and child-care programs will use a variety of supports, such as professional development, parent communication and collaboration, and inclusion incentives, to create a best-practice environment.

This definition is all-encompassing, but what does it really mean? What does it look like in practice? In an inclusive child-care program, children of all ability levels are in the same classroom, and the classroom is age-appropriate even with children mastering different skills. This type of philosophy prevents a program from holding older children back in younger classrooms until they master a certain skill. For example, an inclusive child-care program would allow a three-year-old child to move up to the preschool classroom, even if the child is not yet toilet trained. In a noninclusive classroom, the child may have to stay in the two-year-old classroom until he is completely toilet trained, even if he is almost a year older than the next oldest child in the classroom.

Access

Providing access to all children in the classroom is also important. Obviously, physical access is a key to helping children feel included. This means that children need to be able to move freely through the classroom, the restroom, and the playground. If the program has a child with physical disabilities, staff may need to rearrange the classroom for a child to move from center to center. The playground and bathroom access can be more challenging. Walker or wheelchair ramps may need to be added, and the playground surface needs to be stable so that children with limited mobility do not frequently trip and fall.

Access to the physical space is only one part of the consideration. Children also need to be able to access the classroom materials. There may be some materials that are more challenging for young children to use. For example, if a child has a fine-motor delay, then she may not be able to use a crayon or pencil to begin writing letters. The classroom would need to provide different tools and materials for her to begin learning those skills. She may be able to use a knobbed puzzle to learn letters or make letters out of playdough. Overall, the goal is for the teacher to provide the same content in different methods so that all children have access to learning.

Participation

Inclusion also addresses making children feel like they are part of a learning community and allowing them to participate in the most natural way possible. An overly structured learning environment, in which young children sit in chairs or are required to stay at circle time for an extended period of time, does not allow all children to participate in classroom activities. Even typically developing children have short attention spans and need frequent opportunities to move throughout the day. The classroom needs to form around the abilities of the children. Teachers need to arrange the schedule and the physical classroom design so that children can individually choose their materials based on their interest and length of focus. This type of independence will give children more freedom in the classroom and inspire deeper levels of learning. It will also help children to be more successful at meeting their developmental goals.

Progress

Individual education plans (IEPs) and individual family service plans (IFSPs) outline each year's developmental goals for the children. They help the team of professionals who are supporting the children to monitor their progress. Children with developmental delays and disabilities may not catch up to their same-age peers, but the goal is to show that they are making progress with the support services in place. When teachers document that progress, it shows that children are moving in the right direction and developmental growth is occurring. If no progress is made, or if a child regresses, then the plan is not supporting the child's needs and drastic revisions may be necessary.

Supports

Finally, an inclusive classroom requires supports for the teachers and the administrators. To teach children with a variety of needs, teachers need more extensive training. Most general-education teachers are only given an overview of different disabilities and how to interpret special-education documents. Teachers who must support multiple disabilities each day need training from therapy specialists, medical professionals, and from more experienced teachers. This means that the school administrator must make this type of training a priority for all staff. The administrator also needs to find a way to motivate the staff members. The management of the child-care program needs to find teachers who believe in an inclusive child-care setting and desire that environment for their own classrooms. It is not an easy task to teach in an inclusive classroom, so it is essential for teachers to have all the support possible.

Universal Design for Learning

One way that child-care programs and K–12 schools create inclusive settings is by implementing universal design for learning (UDL). The purpose of UDL is to make sure that every child has the opportunity to be successful in the classroom. This approach creates a flexible learning environment in which the curriculum is shared in different ways, so that students of all ability levels can learn the same information. Children cannot learn in a one-size-fits-all approach, so UDL tries to find multiple methods to teach the same information to help children with perception, engagement, and expression. UDL can also look at ways to create more inclusive workspaces, such as with flexible seating and more accessible playgrounds.

The three main components to universal design for learning (CAST, 2022) include:

- **Representation:** Representation focuses on offering information to children in more than one format. Picture books focus on visual learning, but in an inclusive classroom the teacher should find ways to use text, audio, video, and hands-on learning. In fact, particularly in the early childhood classroom, it is best to start with a hands-on approach to learning to align with a play-based classroom.

- **Expression:** Expression means that a child should be able to express their knowledge in different ways. For example, if a preschool child does not have the fine-motor skills to write his name, then he could use blocks or playdough to make the shapes of the letters.

- **Engagement:** Engagement is the part of UDL that challenges the teacher to motivate children in the classroom. Instead of drilling information and asking for

answers (such as by using flash cards), the teacher is challenged to find new ways to encourage children's learning. This might mean that teacher creates games to teach the children new information or follows the interest of a child to do experiments that trigger their curiosity. This requires the teacher to know what is working in the classroom and what is not and to be creative.

Because the teacher is looking at creative ways to teach all of the students, there is no stigma attached to children who need special education in the classroom. When any educational institution shifts to an inclusive environment, it is important to think about changes in etiquette and respect.

People-First Language vs. Identity-First Language

One way to create a more inclusive classroom and classroom community is to think about how to address individuals with disabilities. Enacted by the Council for the District of Columbia, the People First Respectful Language Modernization Act of 2006 promoted people-first language. The idea behind the act is that an individual should not be identified solely by their disability during a conversation. The person is first, then the condition. For example, instead of saying "an epileptic person," you would say, "a person with epilepsy." This act also encouraged people to stop using outdated terminology such as "mental retardation" or "handicapped."

Although many individuals with disabilities prefer people-first language, some individuals prefer identity-first language (Brown, 2022). Individuals who prefer identity-first language feel strongly that their disability is part of their personality, their temperament, and their whole self. They do not feel that their disability is a characteristic that can be separate from the rest of the person. For example, many adults with autism prefer to be called "autistic" instead of "a person with autism." They may also believe that people-first language signifies that the disability refers to a condition that makes them feel broken or incomplete. In reality, many individuals with disabilities have accepted themselves as a whole, including their disability. They may not want to be referenced in separate parts.

Although how to refer to someone with a disability can be a hot-button topic, the best approach is simply to ask the individual what they prefer. Different people will prefer to be referenced in different ways. Both philosophies have excellent reasoning behind them. It is easy to make an accommodation for someone, once you know what their preference is.

The Etiquette of Respect

Along with learning how to speak to someone with a disability, you should also follow other rules of etiquette when creating an inclusive environment (Easterseals, 2022). One of the keys to disability etiquette is to speak to everyone with respect in an age-appropriate manner. The fact that an individual has a disability does not mean that they should be addressed in a patronizing manner. If you are speaking to an adult with a disability, you should speak to that person like an adult. If you are speaking to a preschool-aged child with a disability, then you should speak to that child like a preschooler, not an infant. That has much to do with the tone of voice that someone is using. Your voice does not need to be high-pitched, bubbly, or in a singsong manner. You do not automatically need to speak more slowly to someone with a disability. If that child or adult does not understand what you are saying, then they can ask for clarification. Many individuals with disabilities, including children with autism or physical disabilities, have no cognitive delays, so there is no reason for you to adapt the way you have a conversation with them.

It is also important that you do not assume that someone with a disability always needs your assistance, even if the individual has a physical disability. It is polite to ask that person if they would like your assistance when opening a door or when carrying something. If the person declines, then they may be confident that they can do it on their own. This is a behavior that we see constantly in young children: "I can do it myself!" A typically developing toddler or preschool student will often want to prove to others that she can handle her task on her own. Children with disabilities will often feel the same way, so an adult should not automatically take away that independence.

WHAT ARE THE BENEFITS OF INCLUSION?

When deciding to make major changes to your child-care program, you must weigh the positives against the negatives. Ultimately, your management team or administration must see that there are significant benefits for the program to change, even if there are financial or administrative barriers to overcome during the process. Becoming an inclusive child-care program will have initial obstacles, but there are considerable benefits for the children, the families, and the program as a whole.

Benefits for the Children

One of the obvious benefits for children with disabilities is that an inclusive child-care program gives them an opportunity that they may not otherwise have; however, there are many more benefits other than an enrollment slot. First, when children are in an inclusive child-care environment, a child's differences may become less noticeable. Many children with disabilities are alienated from peers in daily life. In everyday settings such as birthday parties, gymnastics classes, or worship services, a child with a disability may be the only child present who has a difference. In those settings, the child may be identified by their disability: She is known as the child with the stutter. He is the boy who doesn't play with his classmates. That label begins to follow the child wherever they go. In an inclusive classroom, there is not one type of "typical" child. All children have strengths and weaknesses, and children begin to be identified by strengths: He is the boy who enjoys drawing. She is the girl who always builds block towers. Children deserve a chance to be identified by qualities other than a disability or a shortcoming.

Also, when a child with a disability is pulled out of a traditional classroom setting and placed in an alternative environment, there are usually fewer children in that new environment, and the environment is less diverse. A child may have the chance to become friends with only a handful of other children, and those children may all be diagnosed with similar disabilities. When children are integrated into an inclusive classroom setting, they can make many more friends (EABCC, 2019). They also have the opportunity to build friendships with children who are different from themselves. When children can develop friendships with other children at a young age, it is a pattern they can duplicate for the rest of their lives.

In an inclusive classroom, children with disabilities not only have the option to become friends with their typically developing peers, but they also can also be mentored by those peers (EABCC, 2019). Teachers of any age group of children can tell you how critical it is to have peer role models in the classroom. For example, when a child is told no, they understand to stop a negative behavior, but they don't know what to do instead. When a child sees a peer following directions, it gives them a model for appropriate classroom behavior (EABCC, 2019). Even in preschool, children can learn from positive peer pressure. Children who are struggling with skills such as toilet training, hygiene, and eating at a table during lunch will watch peers and try to model their behavior. An inclusive classroom allows children to learn from both their teacher and their friends.

Children with disabilities also can learn more of the classroom general curriculum when they are in the inclusive classroom. When a child is separated into a different learning environment, often the teacher will focus on the child's deficits instead of working on general curriculum content. A child with disabilities may not be able to master all of the skills that are introduced in the inclusive classroom, but they still have exposure to those skills. Activities in science, math, social studies, music, and other curriculum content may not even be introduced in an isolated special-education environment

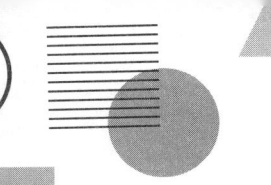

because these environments may only focus on basic skills. Exposure to a range of classroom curricula may make it much easier for the child to learn those skills when he is developmentally ready. An inclusive classroom also allows the child to be exposed to those topics in an age-appropriate manner. This will prevent the child from being introduced to those same topics in later years with cartoonish lessons that are no longer appropriate for the child's age and maturity level.

Since a child with disabilities is introduced to more topics and has the opportunities for more social interactions in the inclusive classroom, it is much more likely that the child will be able to meet their IEP or IFSP goals (EABCC, 2019). For example, if a child with autism is secluded in a special-education classroom with a limited number of students, it will be hard for him to meet the social goals established in an IEP. He needs an opportunity for authentic social interactions with a variety of peers. If he is only exposed to other children with social and emotional delays, then it will be challenging for one child to initiate a social interaction and the other to respond appropriately. In an inclusive classroom, the child will be around students who may initiate a social interaction, and when placed in this situation, he can figure out how to respond. If he can see enough of those social interactions initiated by his typical peers, then he may gain the confidence to start a conversation or play in a group of other children. Even if he only plays beside a group of students who are playing together, he still can observe their group play and learn what it looks like. He would not have those same opportunities in an isolated classroom setting.

When a special-education teacher is responsible for a student who is in an inclusive classroom, then the general classroom teacher and the special-education teacher automatically spend more time collaborating (EABCC, 2019). This is always a benefit for a student with disabilities. Having two professionals with different skill sets working together to develop the best possible education plan is a win-win situation. If the child also sees a therapist or behavior specialist, that person adds additional knowledge and skills to the child's education plan.

This same type of collaboration occurs when the teachers work with the families. Most families of a child with disabilities become natural advocates for their children, and this typically means that they reach out to the teacher more often to make sure the child is getting all the support that she needs. An inclusive classroom allows the family members the opportunity to be involved in the child's education, because by its nature, the classroom has already established the fact that it supports children with disabilities. When the family members and teachers work together on the same strategies and goals, the child is more likely to be successful by having a consistent environment both at home and at school.

Overall, the inclusive classroom allows a child with disabilities to excel by simply being one of the children in the classroom instead of constantly being identified as the "deaf child" or the "disabled child." Having an opportunity to be a regular child, or even to be a child identified by his strengths, can be one of the most freeing experiences that a young child can have.

Benefits for Families

It is difficult to be a child with a disability, but it is also difficult to be the parent of a child with a disability. Parenting a child with different needs can cause a mountain of stress. The family member is constantly worrying if they are making the right decision for the child. This can be even harder when the child is nonverbal or has a cognitive delay that prevents the child from telling the parent how he feels, if he is scared, or if he is hurt. No matter where the family member is, they are constantly worried about whether or not the child is safe and happy.

Because many of the parents and caregivers of children with disabilities must work, child care is essential. Unfortunately, very few child-care programs are accepting of children with disabilities or have staff members trained on how to support children with disabilities (Novoa, 2020). This can leave a parent panicked every time the child is dropped off at child care. As soon as the parent sees the name of the child-care program pop up on her cell phone, she is worried that the child is hurt or is being sent home for the day. Many families of children with disabilities need multiple incomes in the home simply to cover the extra expenses that their child incurs, such as medical bills, therapy visits, medication, or adaptive equipment. That means that every time a child with a disability is suspended or expelled from child care, it puts a parent's job and the family's income at risk (Novoa, 2020).

The largest benefit for families who have a child in an inclusive child-care program is a significant reduction of stress. When a program has stated that its goal is to support children with disabilities, they also make it a goal to keep those children safe and prevent them from being expelled from the program. The parent doesn't have to worry about rearranging their work schedule, taking time off after a suspension, or fighting with a spouse about whose turn it is to stay home from work. Of course, parents of children with disabilities are already more likely to miss work due to additional doctor's appointments or evaluations. Most employers try to take that into consideration and accommodate appointments; however, chronic absenteeism is not accepted at any job. A lack of reliable child care is the biggest contributor to chronic absences at work (Bishop, 2023).

Another benefit for families is that the teachers in inclusive child-care programs typically have a greater knowledge of disabilities (EABCC, 2019). The family can talk to the teachers about symptoms, behaviors, and medication side effects without having to go through the entire history of the disability with every conversation. Even when the child has a less common disability, the program is accustomed to setting up parent-teacher conferences, getting a developmental history of the child, and constantly communicating with the family. Teachers are knowledgeable about how to observe and keep documentation in the classroom. So, if the child begins to demonstrate an unusual behavior or a reaction to medication, then the teachers can share that with the family quickly and the family can seek medical help from a specialist. This goes straight to the heart of keeping the child safe in the classroom. When the teachers understand the child's disability and the typical sequence of child development, they are able to share crucial information with the family. This type of communication system allows the family to feel at ease when they are separated from the child.

Benefits for the Child-Care Program

An inclusive child-care program benefits children with disabilities and their families, but the entire program—including teachers, typically developing students, and the staff—benefits from an inclusive environment as well.

Teachers

When teachers learn to tailor lesson plans for children with disabilities, they learn a valuable skill. Individualizing instruction is key for any classroom. If a teacher is only creating lessons that address the average child's learning needs, children with delays are not the only ones who suffer. Children who are ahead of the developmental curve also need challenging curriculum to advance their own learning.

Differentiated instruction is the practice of modifying lesson plans based on a student's strengths or weaknesses (Wood, 2022). For example, the teacher may be creating a lesson on block play for all the children in the classroom, but she can adapt it based on the students' needs. For children with fine-motor delays, she may focus on helping them pick up the blocks and successfully build a tower that is five blocks tall. For children in the typical development range, she may place toy cars in the block area and encourage the children to build a racetrack. For the students seeking a cognitive challenge, she may encourage them to use the blocks to make ramps and see what characteristics of the ramps make the cars roll the fastest. These individualized steps are still part of the same lesson on blocks, but the steps are different based on the children's needs.

The composition of the classroom encourages the teacher to look at her lesson plan in tiers or phases and to introduce the new phases of the lesson to the children based on their ability levels. As the teacher begins to tier all her lessons, she will see that students who need more challenges are advancing. Students with disabilities are also advancing because they are learning simplified skills one at a time. If a child doesn't have a disability in the fine-motor area, then he may be ready to build the racetrack, even though he has a disability that affects another area of the curriculum. Differentiated instruction allows the teacher to follow the child's needs, and it allows every child in the classroom to advance at their own pace.

Typically Developing Children

Another benefit of an inclusive classroom is that typically developing children can advance their own learning by supporting their peers (EABCC, 2019). In a medical school setting, students are often taught with a "see it, do it, teach it" model of instruction. First, the intern doctor has to observe the procedure. Once the new doctor has observed, it is time to try the procedure on her own. After she has successfully completed the procedure, then it is time for her to teach the procedure to a newer doctor. Maria Montessori used the same model in a multiage preschool classroom. In an inclusive classroom, you have students who are at all three of these stages: see it, do it, and teach it. Once a more advanced student has been able to complete a lesson on his own, he can solidify his own learning by teaching the task to a peer. This can be anything from helping a friend button a vest in the dress-up area to showing a classmate how to do a puzzle. More advanced students can increase their own knowledge and strengthen their skills by assisting other students.

Inclusive environments can teach all children to be respectful of individual differences. The primary focus of most preschool programs is to teach children social and emotional skills that will be with them for the rest of their lives. Children learn to take turns, use kind words, and be respectful of other children and adults. If a child learns these skills in a classroom where all the students have similar characteristics, it is beneficial knowledge; yet, these skills mean so much more when they are taught in an environment where each child looks different, talks differently, and learns differently. It is one thing to learn to be respectful to someone who is just like you. It is a completely different skill set to be respectful to an individual with whom a child appears to have nothing in common.

A diverse classroom setting gives children the opportunity from a young age to learn how to interact with others who are different and to learn that those differences aren't really that significant. As children grow up, they learn many negative words to describe individuals with disabilities. It is easy to use those negative words when they don't actually know someone with a disability. Once a child has a personal relationship with someone, she will be much less likely to want to use a word that could tear down a friend.

An inclusive classroom allows students of all different backgrounds to make friendships. Divisions in classrooms, pull-out groups, and special schools discourage opportunities to create friendships and maintain them over a long period of time. The more that children are kept in the general-education classroom together, the fewer boundaries there are to making friendships. When children are pulled out of the classroom for any reason, such as special education, gifted education, or specialty classes that parents sign their children up for at the child-care program, the less time those children have with the whole group. Children can detect differences at a young age. "Why does Abby get to leave the class for soccer?" "Who is that grownup who takes John away every morning?" When a child doesn't have answers to these types of questions, they begin to create their own theories because they are natural problem-solvers. However, when a child is in the general classroom all day and the therapists come into the classroom and appear to interact with all the children, a greater sense of community is created, where relationships are at the foundation of the classroom.

Staff

Inclusive classrooms can also have a positive impact on the entire staff. Many general-education and early childhood teachers do not have an extensive background in special education. These teachers can learn a great deal when speech pathologists, occupational therapists, physical therapists, and mental-health experts come in to the classrooms to support the children. As the therapists work with the children, they are also teaching the teachers about strategies to use in the classroom. Many of these strategies are also helpful with children who are typically developing. For example, children with autism are not the only ones who have a hard time with social interactions or when the schedule changes. Many children struggle with pronouncing certain words even if they don't have a speech delay. Lots of children are slow to toilet train or learn how to take care of their own hygiene needs, especially if a parent or caregiver doesn't require the child to be independent at home. Learning strategies from an occupational therapist or a speech pathologist can help the teacher to be more successful with all of the children in the classroom.

Learning skills from a specialist can also help the entire staff to be more aware that a child may be struggling with development skills. Not every child with a disability is diagnosed before they enroll in an inclusive classroom. Because inclusive classrooms have trained teachers and typically conduct developmental assessments, they are more likely than noninclusive classrooms to notice children who are struggling to reach developmental milestones. Of course, it is never the teacher's job to diagnose a child with a disability. He can begin to take documentation on usual behaviors or skills that the child is struggling with at school. Sharing this type of documentation with the family and suggesting that the family talk with a pediatrician or another trained professional can help the family address the situation quickly and get support as soon as possible. When all the children enrolled in an inclusive classroom are getting the extra support that they need, the workload can be more manageable for the teachers in the classroom, and the students are more likely to make progress.

Overall, the inclusive classroom has benefits for everyone who is connected to the classroom. The child-care program will develop a reputation for supporting children and families regardless of their background, and that is a reputation that the community will highly value. It is also the type of reputation that attracts funders and volunteers. Supporting every child, regardless of their ability, is the best practice, regardless of the circumstances.

A Parent's Perspective

The following is the story of parents and their search for inclusive child care. Note: Some parts of the story may be disturbing.

I met my sons for the first time in the emergency room of the local university hospital. My wife and I received a phone call at two in the morning from the foster care caseworker asking if we could handle the emergency placement of an infant and a toddler. We had only been approved to be foster parents for about a month. We had prepared our home for an infant and specifically had asked for an infant whose birth parents had terminated all parental rights. The social worker told us that we may have to wait a while for that particular circumstance, but she was hoping we would be willing to host other foster children in the meantime due to the overwhelming demand for foster parents in our state.

The social worker met us in the waiting room at the ER, and she told us that we needed to prepare ourselves before we met the boys. They had been removed from an abusive setting, and their injuries were overwhelming to see. Joshua was almost two years old, and his brother, Amal, was eleven months younger. Amal was covered in bruises and cigarette burns, and there was an imprint of a belt buckle on his lower back. He was only eleven months old, and he had already seen more violence than most adults see in a lifetime. Joshua was also covered in bruises, and he also had a bright blue cast on his right arm. The social worker told us that his mother's boyfriend had twisted his small arm as a punishment and had caused a spiral fracture. The boys were malnourished. Their faces were gaunt, and they sat on the hospital bed eating cup after cup of hospital Jell-o.

My wife and I took turns staying home with the boys while they healed. We both worked for large companies that made it possible for us to take intermittent leave through the Family Medical Leave Act (FMLA). During those two months, we searched for child-care programs that could take a one-year-old and a two-year-old. Some centers had room for one of the boys but not the other. Of course, we wanted them together for convenience, but we also thought it was necessary to keep them together to ease their transition into a new home and help them feel safe. Finally, a center called us and said that they had spots available for both boys. The program wasn't close to our home, but it was the only program that had offered us spots. We agreed to take the spots with the idea that we were still on other waiting lists, so something better for the family could eventually come along.

When the boys started at the first private child-care program, we let the center director and the teachers know that they were our foster children and had only been with us for a little over two months. We decided not to go into detail about how horrific their birth home had been unless it became necessary later. We wanted the program to understand that they were going through a big transition, but we didn't want to upset others with the graphic details. The birth parents did not have visitation rights, so the boys were acclimating to new parents. The teachers told us to expect the first couple of weeks to be tough since the boys were experiencing another major change, but they also told us that children are tough and usually show more resilience than adults.

During the first month, the teachers seemed sympathetic. We received reports about the boys hitting peers, crying during naptime, or refusing to follow directions. We were also told that these were all normal behaviors for children experiencing the types of changes that the boys were experiencing. Joshua wouldn't sleep at naptime, and that seemed to really frustrate the teachers. His primary teacher told me that she would try to rub his back to calm him down, but he would continue to cry. I told her that he was afraid of the dark and cried at night also. At that point I started to give her a few details about his past and explained that he might have nightmares when he sleeps. She seemed to take that into consideration, but she also told me that teachers must clean the room during naptime and that he needed to rest.

Amal began struggling in his classroom also. Whenever another child approached him, he would bite the child. Out of everything the teachers complained about, the biting seemed to be the issue that they just couldn't handle. They also seemed to think that our eleven-month-old son was purposely biting other children just to be mean. We began receiving little template letters each day that documented each time he bit a classmate. Other children would receive a photocopied letter saying that they had been bitten. The letters never said who was involved in the biting, but they were set out on the counter at pick-up time. A parent who received a notification saying that their child had been bitten could easily look around to see which child had a note stating he or she was the biter. The other parents in Amal's classroom quickly figured out that he was biting the other children, and that made our appearances at the school uncomfortable.

When my wife or I arrived in the classroom in the evening, we would be greeted by a college student who worked part-time in the afternoons after the lead teacher had left for the day. She never knew the details of most of the incidents, but she would basically shame us for the number of times that Amal had bitten the other children. I would cry the entire ride home from the school because I felt so helpless in the situation. I wasn't with Amal during the day to intercede between him and his classmates, but I was being held responsible for his actions.

This daily tension was too much for my wife. One morning, she decided to drop the boys off at school early so that she could speak with the center director before she went to work. When she arrived, the director said that she was glad Carrie had stopped by because she was going to call us. The director began to discuss the number of biting incidents that had occurred since Amal had enrolled in the program. She also told us that she was implementing a new biting policy with a point system in order to protect all the children in the center. A child would be given points for bites and more points for bites that broke the other child's skin. After three months, points would drop off the child's record. The way the system was set up, it seemed like Amal had three to four days before the center could expel him. Carrie called me after she left the director's office and said that we needed to call other centers immediately to make sure that we had child care waiting. Each

of us had a small amount of FMLA left, but pretty soon we would have to be docked pay for missing work.

My stomach began to hurt each day after lunch as I dreaded pick-up time. On the third day, the college student told me that I needed to speak with the director before I picked up the boys. The director did not expel Amal, but she told me that she really thought the boys needed a nanny. She said they couldn't provide the type of care they needed. I asked her if Joshua still had a spot in his classroom, and she said that the center wasn't a good fit for "our family." We were the only same-sex couple with children enrolled in the child-care program, and we were the only family whose children were a different ethnicity than their parents. The boys also had strong behaviors, but it seemed odd that our entire family was being asked to leave. I wondered if her choice was based on her policy or on discrimination.

I left the child-care center that night with all of my boys' belongings in tow, and I desperately tried to make it home before I started crying. Joshua was old enough that he could ask me basic questions about why I was upset, and I did not want my boys to think I was upset with them. I needed to focus on finding a new child-care program and resuming a normal routine as soon as possible. Another major disruption, like a change in where the boys spend nine hours each day, was going to be even harder on them. I just wanted to make things stable again as soon as possible.

I talked with a couple of child-care programs the next morning and learned quickly that I should not mention that Amal was a biter. Directors always asked me if the boys had been in child care before and why we had left our previous program. I felt like some of the directors knew my name when I called to ask about enrollment. Were the directors talking to each other about us? Surely they had better things to do. It took another three weeks, but we found a center that had just expanded and was opening a new classroom. They had room for Joshua, and they would be able to start Amal in just a few weeks. We had to go ahead and start paying for Amal's spot even though he wasn't attending yet, but it seemed worth it if we knew we had secure child care in the near future.

The program asked us to come in for a tour and bring the boys so that the teachers could meet them before they started. This seemed like a good way to help the boys transition. We were up-front with the center director about the trauma in the boys' past so that the staff members would understand any negative behaviors that came up. During the tour, Amal bit his brother on the arm when Joshua accidentally bumped into him and knocked him to the ground. The director asked me if this happened often, and I explained that it occasionally occurred when Amal felt stressed or threatened. She took that opportunity to explain the center's biting policy. She said that the center did not expel children for biting. I was overjoyed the second I heard this! Then, she told me that if a child bit three times in one day, he or she would be sent home for the remainder of the day. This information was a little bit harder to hear. Amal did not bite three times every day, but there were days when he had. If he bit three times at the beginning of the day, then would we have to leave work early on a regular basis? How would we rotate who stayed home? Carrie's company was more flexible than mine, but she was a supervisor and needed to be there to oversee her team. This could be complicated. After we got home and put the boys to bed, we decided to rotate back and forth for the time being, especially since we didn't know how frequently this would be a problem. We were basically hoping for the best but expecting the worst.

During our first month at our new program, Amal seemed to do well. There were lots of days where he bit two times, but he hadn't been sent home yet. The other parents in his classroom had figured out that he was the biter, especially since the increase in biting started when he joined the class. There was judgment from the other parents and the other teachers, but we had lived through that before.

We had spent so much time in the previous several months worrying about Amal and his biting that we hadn't really worried about how Joshua was doing. He was a typical first child, trying to help us as much as possible, even though he was still in the two-year-old classroom. He frequently told us that he was a "big boy" and that he wanted to be a helper. We had focused our attention on other places, and then we realized how much Joshua was struggling.

The first issue that we heard about at school was that Joshua wouldn't take a nap and cried at naptime when the lights were off. We explained to the teachers that he had experienced past trauma and had nightmares when he went to sleep. They told us that they were sympathetic to what he had been through, but they did not make any changes to the classroom expectations. All children are required to stay on their mats during the two-hour naptime, and children are supposed to go to sleep. We asked if he could have toys or books on his mat so that he would stay there, but the teacher told us that was unfair to the children who were sleeping like they were supposed to be.

She also said that as children begin to wake up each day, then they would want to have toys as well. Each day, we received a teacher's note with a sad face on it that said Joshua hadn't slept at naptime. I asked the teacher what she wanted me to do to help. She said that I needed to tell him naptime was for sleeping. I explained that I could try that, but as an adult, I couldn't sleep when I wasn't tired either.

The teacher also began to tell us that Joshua was not following directions during circle time. The teacher was upset that Joshua would not sit "crisscross applesauce" during circle time and he never stopped moving or bothering his friends. I asked her to explain to me what happened during a normal circle time, and she began to get upset and explain that her circle time was just like all the other classroom circle times, and she wasn't doing anything out of the ordinary. Joshua was now in a classroom of older two-year-old and younger three-year-old children. I kept thinking that his classroom circle time shouldn't be the same as the students preparing for kindergarten next year, but maybe I was wrong since I didn't really have any training with young children (other than foster-parent training). After I continued to ask questions about Joshua's behavior in relation to the other children in the classroom, the director and the teacher agreed that I could observe the class circle time one morning.

The classroom shared a supply closet with an adjoining classroom. The closet had a window through which I could peek so that Joshua wouldn't see me. I observed the teacher and the teacher assistant continually reprimanding Joshua for not wanting to tear down his tower of blocks to go to circle time, for not sitting "correctly" during circle time, and for accidentally bumping a child when he wiggled around. He received a sad face by his name on the behavior chart. Then he was reprimanded for not lining up properly when it was time to go outside. I was hoping I could figure out why Joshua was struggling, but what I did see confused me even more.

The teacher initially invited all the children to circle time by flashing the lights on and off. Then, all the children began cleaning up their toys. Joshua was in the middle of building a huge block tower, and you could tell that he didn't want to clean up. He got a warning from the assistant teacher when most of the children were done cleaning up and he had not yet started. When all the other children had arrived at circle time, Joshua was still standing by his block tower, and it was obvious that he did not want to join circle time if it meant he had to tear down his tower. The assistant teacher came over and told him that if he didn't take down the tower, she would. He began to cry, but he slowly disassembled his tower.

When Joshua arrived at circle time, he already seemed defeated. The teacher told all the children to stand up to do several dances. Joshua did not want to stand up and dance, so the teacher reprimanded him again for not participating. He stood up, but he did not engage like the other students. When the class sat back down, the teacher began to lead calendar time with the assistance of a student helper. The students sang a song about the months of the year and the teacher counted all thirty days on the calendar. Joshua began to wiggle. His legs where crossed when he first sat down, but now he was rocking back and forth. Then, he rolled over onto his stomach. The teacher stopped circle time to tell him that he wasn't sitting correctly.

Circle time took about ten minutes, and then it was time for the teacher to read. She sat three books down beside her and then picked up the first one to read. The first story took about eight minutes. It didn't seem like Joshua paid attention to a word of the story, but he was sitting at the circle and not touching other students. I thought that was a success, and I was hoping she would dismiss the children to play. Instead, she picked up a second book and began to read. Joshua struggled during this story. He rocked back and forth like he was trying to keep himself awake. That caused him to bump into other students, resulting in more reprimands from the teacher. At that point, the teacher said "Joshua, please go move your name to the sad face." I turned my gaze and noticed a posterboard-sized paper with all the children's names on it. Beside each name was a happy face and a sad face. There was Velcro on the back of the children's names. Joshua pulled his name off the poster and placed it on the spot with the sad face.

I could not believe that my son was humiliated like this. I was furious. Again, Joshua just looked defeated. He went back to the circle and sat in his spot while the teacher began reading a third book. At this point, I noticed that another student had fallen asleep in circle time while sitting straight up and bobbing her head toward her chest. Joshua was not the only student struggling with this teaching style, but he was wiggling and bumping students in the process. The teacher didn't mind the sleeping child because she wasn't bothering anyone else. Finally, circle time was over, and the teacher began asking students to individually line up at the door to go out to the playground. All the students lined up, except for Joshua. The teacher talked to him about his poor behavior during circle time and told him that he had to sit on the bench on the playground for ten minutes: five minutes for not cleaning up and five minutes for disturbing his friends at circle time.

I left the closet and went to the director's office. I told her about the several things that worried me: the behavior chart, the length of circle time, and forcing Joshua to take apart his tower. The director told me that the preschool wing of the center was now working to prepare children for kindergarten and that I needed to realize what would be expected of my son in elementary school. I responded that he had two full years to prepare, and he didn't need to be ready for kindergarten today. She told me that we could set up a conference with the teacher to discuss my concerns, but that I shouldn't expect the teachers to change the entire classroom for my child because public school would definitely not make those kinds of drastic changes for us.

Carrie and I waited for the parent-teacher conference, but while we waited, Amal was sent home again for biting three times. This time he bit all three times early in the day and was sent home before lunch. Carrie left work early to pick him up and worked from home the following day. The next day the same thing happened again; I left work early and picked him up. After the third day in a row, I wondered if he was old enough to have figured out this trick. He bites, is sent to the office, and then he gets to go home. It started to happen almost every day. Carrie and I began fighting over who should stay home. It wasn't as easy as rotating when it came to factoring in important presentations, staff evaluations, or business trips. It seemed like every day I could count on a phone call from the child-care program in the morning and a fight with Carrie in the evening. Both of us were worried about the possibility of losing our jobs, so we both had reason for frustration.

One day when the director called me to pick up Amal early, I asked her if she had found a date for our conference with Joshua's teacher. She told me to come talk to her when I came to the center. When I arrived, I went to her office, but she didn't want to talk about a parent-teacher conference. Instead, she said that it was time to "stop kidding ourselves" and realize that her center was not the right program for my sons. She continued to say that she had multiple families threatening to leave the child-care program if Amal continued to be enrolled. She also said that she did not believe that Joshua was learning in his classroom since he would not follow directions or participate in circle time. She told me that she would give me until the end of the week so that we could find alternate arrangements, but it was already

Wednesday, so two days was not going to help us find the care we needed. I told her that we would not be back the following day.

That night, after we put the boys to bed, Carrie and I had a huge fight. We argued about who was going to stay home with the boys. We fought about whether or not our boys were capable of being in a child-care program. We stressed over the possibility of whether or not we could afford a private nanny instead of using group child care. I even suggested maybe we weren't the best family to raise the boys if this is the life that they would have with us. I can't believe I said it out loud. I felt like I had betrayed Carrie, the boys, and our family. We were still fostering. Maybe another family would be more equipped to deal with boys who had experienced so much trauma in their past. Maybe the centers were being harder on us for being a two-mother family, and a traditional family would help the boys get more of the supports that they needed. Carrie told me that she had thought some of the same things too, but those thoughts were going to be banished from future conversations. The four of us were a family now, and if we experienced discrimination, we were going to overcome it together. That did seem very comforting when she said it out loud. We had figured out one problem, but the biggest problem was still hovering over us. I talked to my mother the next morning. She lived four hours away, but she agreed to come stay with us for a week or two as a stopgap to figure out our plan of action.

The next day at work, a co-worker told me about a child-care program in our town that focused on working with children with disabilities. The center was able to serve all children, but they reserved a portion of the slots for children with disabilities. The program had been in our town for more than thirty years. The co-worker said that the program also had pediatric therapy in the same building. Children enrolled in the program could be evaluated for therapy, and if they qualified, the therapists would come and work with them in their classrooms during the school day. I thought, surely my boys would graduate from high school before they could get a spot in a program like this. My colleague said that the program had just expanded and moved to a bigger building. They had doubled the program size and were trying to fill the new spots as quickly as possible. I asked to leave work immediately. Instead of calling, I decided to drive there and talk to someone face-to-face. I thought if the administrator could see the desperation in my face, surely, she would know how badly my family needed this opportunity.

When I arrived at the building, I walked in to find the administration desk, but what caught my eye was a large room that had strange swings and climbing devices all over it. It was larger than a classroom. During my tour, the director told me that the room was a therapy gym for children receiving occupational therapy or physical therapy. When I viewed the classrooms, I saw that there were fewer children than I had anticipated. I asked the director if that was because they still hadn't reached maximum capacity. She said that those classrooms were already full. The one-year-old room had a maximum capacity of eight children, and the two-year-old room had a maximum capacity of twelve children. I was astounded. The two-year-old room at our last center had twenty children in it.

As we viewed the rest of the building, I did not hear any teacher yell. I saw infants being played with on the classroom floor and one-year-olds doing art projects. The teachers were playing with the children on the playground instead of watching them while they rested on a bench. There was a playground for infants and toddlers and a separate playground for the preschoolers. The director told me that every lead teacher had at least a four-year degree in education or child development, and she said that the therapists worked with the teachers to train them on how to support the children. The price was high for a child-care program, but it was not even close to the cost of a nanny. I signed the enrollment paperwork and paid our deposit before I left that day.

The director gave me paperwork for each of the boys to fill out about their temperament, likes, and dislikes. After I discussed their history with her, she also gave me forms to fill out to have them screened for any developmental delays. I thought that maybe the screening would give us time before the center decided to kick them out, but she didn't seem to think that would be an issue. This was our third child care in one year. Every transition seemed like it was getting harder, so I wasn't ready to believe her just yet. That night, Carrie didn't even care that I had signed up the boys without talking to her first. She was thrilled that we had found someplace that might be more open-minded.

During the first two weeks at the new program, one of the occupational therapists called us and asked us to come in to talk about Amal. She said that she thought his excessive biting had to do with some issues involving his sensory system and some struggles using his language to communicate with his peers. She asked for permission to have Amal's hearing and speech evaluated. She also gave us some ideas on how to help Amal in the classroom. She showed us vibrating teethers and ice pops that he could use in the classroom to take in more sensory information without hurting his friends. She also gave us developmental information from an organization called Zero to Three to explain why biting was normal for toddlers. She gave us another handout from a national occupational therapists' organization that talked about biting that was happening more often than is typically seen.

The teacher and assistant teacher created a learning plan for Amal and talked about the kind of therapy that they would use in the classroom to prevent him from biting others. Once the insurance information was processed, the occupational therapist (OT) began to see Amal once a week in his classroom, and she would occasionally pull him out one-on-one to work in the therapy gym. If Amal was having a hard day, one of the OTs or an OT college practicum student would take him on a walk in the building or swing him in the therapy gym to help him calm down. The biting didn't stop completely, but it seemed to be more like the normal biting described in the Zero to Three handout.

Joshua was also getting accustomed to a new classroom. He had a therapy evaluation also, and it showed delays in speech and physical development. The therapist told us there were also some issues with his sensory system, but they were different from Amal's needs. Although Joshua also qualified for weekly speech and occupational therapy, it didn't seem as noticeable in his new classroom. The teacher invited me to come observe the classroom after the first couple of weeks, and I immediately noticed differences from his old classroom.

Circle time lasted less than fifteen minutes, and the children were able to sit at circle time in any position they wanted. Every child had a rectangular carpet square, and as long as they stayed on their carpet square, it didn't matter what position they were in. I also noticed one child that wandered around the back of the classroom during circle. No one ever forced him to come and sit down. I don't know what the child's personal situation was, but I was comforted to know that he had that freedom. After their circle time, the class went out to the playground. Every child went out to play, and I never saw a child sitting in time out on the playground. In fact, I even noticed that the surface of the playground allowed a little girl in a wheelchair to come out and participate with the rest of the class. Every child was getting to play and be a kid.

There were no behavior charts in the classroom. When a child got frustrated, I noticed the teachers reacted quickly and interceded before someone was hit. The smaller class size seemed to help. Of course, there were children who did hit or bite. When I saw a child display aggressive behavior, it was almost a seamless process: one teacher immediately went to comfort the child who was hurt; the other teacher removed the child who was frustrated to an area away from the other children. In some cases, the teacher thought the child needed a break from the room and called the therapy office for help. In other cases, the teacher talked to the child about why their action hurt. Then she asked the child to find a different area to play in until they were calm. I never saw a typical time-out, but the child was still told that was not an acceptable behavior. More than anything else, I learned that I trusted these teachers with my children.

It was still a child-care program, so there were times that I noticed a teacher didn't stay at the center very long, particularly the college students who helped work in the afternoon. Working with young children is a hard job, so someone shouldn't do it if they don't feel equipped. I was grateful that our lead teachers stayed the same. I heard them talk about things that I don't think our other centers had, like planning time. It also seemed like the administration and the parents did a lot to celebrate the teachers and make them feel appreciated.

We still got phone calls about Amal and Joshua. We had to come in for conferences or to meet with the therapists. The biggest difference was that the school seemed to be working with us for the benefit of both children. When we first started looking for child care, we had no idea that there were child-care programs that couldn't support our children. The problem is that very few places offer the type of child care that we found. It is hard work to support children and families this way, but it truly is making a huge difference in the life of our family.

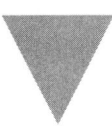

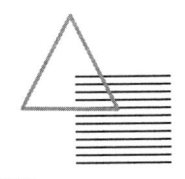

CHAPTER 2

Laws Surrounding Special Education

Families of children with disabilities frequently ask whether a center is required by law to serve their children. There are laws that prevent discrimination against individuals with disabilities and laws that guarantee a child with a disability the right to an equitable education. However, not all of these laws apply to every child-care program. When a program partners with Head Start or a state-funded preschool, then it receives funding that makes it responsible for following these laws, so it is important for child-care programs to understand their legal responsibilities with regard to serving all children.

Many centers have had to tell a family that the program does not have the resources to serve their child. Typically, this is not due to an issue of discrimination. In fact, many centers would love to serve every child who attempts to enroll in their programs. Often the centers will decline enrollment or tell the family that the child needs other care arrangements because of the center's own lack of resources. If a private child-care center is operating on the minimum state requirements, with large adult-to-child ratios, then the staff may not be able to give more individualized care to a child who has a disability. The director or administrator and staff may be worried about legal liability if the child gets hurt, wanders off, or hurts others. Without some of the government supports that the public school system receives, the center may not be able to provide the safe care that the child needs. Leaders of child-care programs often imagine how many children they could serve with expanded funding. Some programs partner with foundations or receive grants to support children who need extra resources, but donations are not the only way to support children with disabilities.

A child-care center that partners with a federal Head Start program or a state-funded preschool program receives the funding needed to support children with disabilities and may have a legal obligation to serve all children with disabilities who apply and enroll. The key difference in service availability is the funding stream. Different funding streams have different obligations, and a stronger funding stream can better support a high-quality environment for children with disabilities. All child-care programs, and businesses in general, are required to make some accommodations for individuals with disabilities, but those universal accommodations may be focused more on facility updates than on educational supports. Overall, it is important for program administrators and families of children with disabilities to understand the laws that protect Americans with disabilities and know how they apply to child care.

In this chapter, you'll learn about the following laws and how they may affect your child-care program and the children you serve:

- Americans with Disabilities Act of 1990
- Individuals with Disabilities Education Improvement Act of 2004
- Section 504 of the Rehabilitation Act
- Health Insurance Portability and Accountability Act of 1996

The chapter concludes with a discussion about how families can use the legal system to ensure that their children with disabilities are receiving the care they need.

AMERICANS WITH DISABILITIES ACT

The Americans with Disabilities Act of 1990 (ADA) is a law intended to curb discrimination against people with disabilities. The act prohibits discrimination with regard to employment, transportation, communications, public accommodations, and access to state and federal government services and resources. The ADA focuses on making all buildings and services accessible to Americans with disabilities (US Department of Labor, 2022).

The US Department of Education enforces Title II of ADA. Title II is the portion that prevents state and local governments, including the public school system, colleges, and universities, from discriminating against individuals with disabilities. The act does not specifically list all the conditions covered by the law, so it can be a little vague. In a child-care program, this law may mean that a facility must provide a wheelchair ramp for a child or a parent with a disability. It could also mean that a program may need to provide an interpreter for a child or a family member who is hearing impaired when the child-care program hosts a parent education night.

As an independent business funded by family payments or community grants, the child-care program would still have a great deal of freedom in how the educational curriculum is designed, as long as it meets the state's minimum standards for licensure. The program could create its own plan for supports for children with diagnosed disabilities and would not be required to meet the Individuals with Disabilities Education Act (IDEA) standards because it does not receive state or federal funding.

INDIVIDUALS WITH DISABILITIES EDUCATION ACT

The Individuals with Disabilities Education Improvement Act (IDEA), Parts B and C, is a law that ensures a free and appropriate public education (FAPE) to all students in the public school system (20 USC 1400, 2004; US Department of Education, n.d.a.). It is not an anti-discrimination law. Children between the ages of three and twenty-one years receive services through IDEA, Part B, and infants and toddlers through thirty-six months of age receive early intervention through IDEA, Part C. President Gerald Ford initially established the law in 1975 as the Education for All Handicapped Children Act with four primary purposes:

- To provide special-education services to all children who needed them
- To maintain equitable services for all children with disabilities
- To implement a uniform evaluation system for all children receiving special education
- To provide federal resources to the public school system to educate children with disabilities

In 1990, it changed to the Individuals with Disabilities Education Act (IDEA) and was most recently reauthorized in 2004 and amended in 2015. IDEA gives specific details on the disabilities that it supports, which include:

- Autism
- Deaf-blindness
- Deafness
- Emotional disturbance
- Hearing impairment
- Intellectual disability
- Multiple disabilities
- Orthopedic impairments
- Other health impairments
- Specific learning disabilities

- Speech or language impairment
- Traumatic brain injury
- Visual impairment, including blindness

(US Department of Education, n.d.a.).

IDEA attempts to provide as much time as possible for students to be in a general-education classroom with needed supports, instead of isolating them in a special-education classroom (US Department of Education, n.d.a.). Special supports are provided for children when a disability interferes with a child's ability to be successful in the classroom. If a student's disability does not affect their ability to learn and receive equitable school services, then the school system will not provide special supports. For example, a child could have a physical disability, such as using a prosthetic limb. If that disability does not affect the child's ability to be successful in the classroom, then she would not need special supports. However, if the child's prosthetic arm requires the help of a para-educator to take notes in class, or if she needs a special-education teacher to assist her with using technology to overcome her disability, then a special-education plan would be needed.

A child between the ages of three and twenty-one years who qualifies for special-education services must be provided with an individualized education program (IEP). The IEP must include the child's strengths; the family's concerns about the child's abilities to learn in school; the results of the most recent evaluation; and the academic, developmental, and functional needs of the child (20 USC 1400, 2004). The IEP must be re-evaluated annually, and the goals must be adjusted according to the child's classroom performance and most recent evaluation. The child must have an evaluation every three years, so the annual IEP may be using an evaluation that is a year or two old. If the child is younger than three years of age, then he or she will have an individualized family service plan (IFSP) to determine needed therapy through home visits and to determine the developmental goals for the child with the support of the therapy. This plan will also be re-evaluated annually (20 USC 1400. 2004).

Along with setting developmental goals for the child, the IEP or ISFP specifies the least restrictive environment (LRE) for the student (Department of Education, n.d.a.). This means that, to the extent possible, children with disabilities will be educated with children who are typically developing, in public or private institutions. The school is guided to use special classes, separate schools, or removing students from typical settings only when the severity of the child's disability requires a different environment for learning. For example, a student with a disability may spend 80 percent of the school day in a typical classroom setting but may be pulled out of the classroom to receive individualized speech therapy or for a developmental assessment, if the classroom conditions prevent him from focusing for those specific learning experiences.

The IDEA law also secures a FAPE for all children three years of age and older with a diagnosed need for special education. This means that the public school system is responsible for providing that free and appropriate education, but it does not necessarily mean that it will be provided in a public school building. Many states across the United States are implementing a mixed-delivery service model for free preschool. If a public school system does not have enough facility space or teaching staff to serve all the children who qualify for services, they may implement a *mixed-delivery* system, meaning that the public school system can offer funding to private child-care programs so they can provide an education equivalent to what is offered in the public school system. When the public school system partners with a private child-care program and uses state and federal funds to support services in the child-care classrooms, then the child-care program is also responsible for complying with IDEA.

The law also ensures that the public school system will try to find children with disabilities and make sure that they are given special education services (Department of Education, n.d.a.). This process is called Child Find. Public school districts must have a plan to find and identify children with disabilities and evaluate them so that they can receive the IEPs and IFSPs that they need to be successful in the classroom.

Public-private partnerships can be important to child-care providers and families. Many public school preschool programs offer only half-day services, and working families need care and education for the remainder of the day for their children. Many child-care programs offer ten to twelve hours of care a day to accommodate working families, so a family may prefer to be in a mixed-delivery child-care site where the child can receive the benefits of IDEA funding but can also receive a full day of care. Child-care programs are limited in what they can charge families by the amount the families can afford to pay. That means that many child-care programs operate at higher adult-to-child ratios than they would prefer, but they must do so to remain open. When the public school system supports the program with special-education funding, then the program can afford to hire highly qualified teachers and have lower teacher-to-child ratios. This means better care for all the children enrolled in the program.

Child-care programs that are privately funded still have the opportunity to offer inclusive environments, but they are not legally obligated to follow the requirements of the IDEA. A child's family still can apply to their local school district to receive an IEP or IFSP for their child, and the school system can provide select therapy, such as weekly speech and language therapy. The family then can share that plan with the private child-care program, and the center can support the child's developmental goals as best as possible. The family can also pursue private pediatric therapy and have the therapist collaborate with the child-care program. Some inclusive child-care programs even have their own therapists on-site to make the child-care program full service for the children enrolled.

Another aspect of the IDEA is requiring confidentiality of all children's records. The Family Educational Rights and Privacy Act (FERPA) ensures confidentiality with regard to a child's diagnosis, treatment, and student records. Confidentiality applies to both IDEA Parts B and C. The parents of the child should have more access and control over the records, and the school is obligated to keep records confidential and unidentifiable (Department of Education, n.d.a.). This law can affect child-care providers in two different ways. First, if the program is partnering with a preschool based in a public school, then the program is obligated to maintain the highest levels of confidentiality regarding the students' personal information. Of course, this practice should be maintained ethically in all education settings, but IDEA makes it a legal offense if the child-care program does not abide by it.

Second, if the child-care program is operating solely as a private business that is trying to support children enrolled who also attend a public school preschool program, then it can be difficult to obtain records on the student to further support the child's growth. The easiest way to see a child's IEP or IFSP is to partner with the family and ask whether the child-care program can see a copy of the child's developmental goals, so that the classroom teacher at the program can work on the same goals as the school system. If the child-care program reaches out to the school system itself to request the records, then the program would have to get waivers signed by the family stating that the center may share information with the school and the school will share information with the center. This practice is usually reserved for medical professionals who may be contributing to the child's IEP or IFSP. Most school systems prefer to refer the child-care program back to the family.

SECTION 504 OF THE REHABILITATION ACT

Section 504 of the Rehabilitation Act of 1973 is a federal law that protects the rights of qualified individuals (including children) from discrimination based on their disability (US Department of Health and Human Services, Office for Civil Rights. 2006). Again, it prevents any business or organization from discriminating against an individual with a disability if the business receives any federal funding. If a child in a public school has a disability, then that child is entitled to a 504 plan, which allows accommodations for children with disabilities to help them be successful in a typical classroom setting. It may mean that a child needs additional time for a test or requires movement breaks throughout the day if that child cannot sit still for an extended period of time. Many children with 504 plans have a medical disability such as asthma, attention-deficit hyperactivity disorder (ADHD), or epilepsy. They may need accommodations such as taking medication during the school day or being exempt from physical activities that may aggravate their condition. A 504 plan does not provide special-education classes or support therapies like an IEP does, but it can provide accommodations that many students need. For example, a student in a wheelchair may need the classroom to be rearranged so that she is able to move through the room more freely. She may also need appropriate materials placed on lower shelves so that she can select them independently. A student with epilepsy may struggle with the lighting on the computer screen if he has photosensitive epilepsy, so he may need the same type of content placed in a board game instead of a computer game.

HEALTH INSURANCE PORTABILITY AND ACCOUNTABILITY ACT OF 1996

Most individuals are familiar with the Health Insurance Portability and Accountability Act of 1996, better known as HIPAA. This is not an educational law; however, HIPAA may apply to child-care programs that interact with a child's medical records, for example, if a child receives outpatient therapy on-site at the child-care facility (CDC, 2022). Inclusive child-care programs that provide pediatric therapy on-site must keep children's records confidential and make sure that there is no identifiable information in a child's educational files that can be decoded by outside individuals. Most inclusive child-care programs that offer therapy also work with health insurance companies, so they may have a medical billing specialist on staff who handles HIPAA-related tasks. Even if the facility only takes cash payments, it still must make sure that medical records and coding meet the HIPAA standards to ensure patient confidentiality.

DUE-PROCESS HEARINGS

If a child with a disability is not getting the special-education services that his family believes he needs and deserves, then the family has a right to a due-process hearing. A due-process hearing is almost like a court case, and it is based on whether the child is getting a FAPE. The family can contest the child's evaluation, diagnosis, placement, and implementation of services. This dispute is typically with the public school system, but if a child-care program is part of a mixed-delivery model where the public school sends children to the child-care program, then the child-care program could also be involved in the hearing. Ultimately, the school system will have to prove that the child is getting the best possible education based on the child's evaluation and diagnosis. If the family disputes the evaluation or diagnosis, then the family can provide documentation from professionals outside the public school system that state a difference of opinion.

An impartial hearing officer is appointed to preside over the case. The school system is typically represented by their legal counsel, so families can feel overwhelmed when dealing with the legal jargon as they advocate for the rights of their child. Parents may need to seek a special-education attorney to get the best representation possible. Ultimately, parents are very knowledgeable about their own children, so it is important for the school system to listen to their concerns. Parents must also be reasonable about what the child needs and the actual severity of the disability. If the family doesn't like the manner in which the public school system attempts to support the child, the family has the option to withdraw the child and find alternative education. If the school is not providing a free and appropriate education, then the school system is at fault, and the child's IEP must be updated.

Even if a child-care program is a privately funded business, it is still possible that family members may take legal action against the program if they feel that their child with a disability is being discriminated against. In this case, the family may be seeking legal action under the protection of the ADA. If a family takes any type of legal action, it is essential for the child-care program to seek legal counsel that specializes in that type of law. Just because the program is not required to meet the requirements of IDEA does not mean that the family could not make a case for discrimination. Ultimately, the best practice for any child-care program is to support all children in the classroom to the best of its ability and to partner with the parents to make the environment safe and successful. If the child's needs are greater than the supports that the program can offer, it is best to have an honest conversation with the family. A strong communication system and great parent partnerships will help the child and benefit the center as a whole.

CHAPTER 3

Vision and Mission Statements

A child-care program is not just an educational institution; it is also a small business established for a specific purpose. For a child-care program to achieve the objectives that the board or the owner intends, they must establish priorities and determine which principles will be most important to the business when making key decisions. This is especially important for an inclusive child-care program because families and staff members must understand that the program has a unique goal to serve all children. Two of the primary guiding documents for any business or school are a vision statement and a mission statement.

CREATING A VISION STATEMENT

A vision statement is much shorter than a mission statement. It may only be two to three sentences long, but it summarizes the overarching goals of the child-care program. To write the vision statement, the school leadership really needs to think about the long-term goals of the school. What does the school want to be known for in the community? What type of relationship does the program want to have with families? Whom is the child-care program meant to serve?

Even if the goal of the vision statement is lofty, the vision statement itself should be clear and succinct. It does not need to go into great detail, because the mission statement can do that. The vision statement is meant to be an idealistic articulation of what the administration wants the program to stand for and accomplish in the future. The vision statement is also a guidepost that will help investors decide whether the program aligns with organizations they choose to support financially.

Here are a few tips to help businesses shape a new vision statement:

1. Keep it short. It should not be longer than three sentences.

2. Avoid using jargon specific to the child-care field. Make sure that anyone can read and understand the vision statement, not just those in the same field.

3. Do not use metaphors. A vision statement should not be open to interpretation. Any audience should be able to read it and understand the same message.

4. It should define what makes the business unique from others so that it only applies to that individual organization.

5. It should be optimistic and ambitious so that it will inspire those who work at the child-care program and those in the community who want to learn more about it.

6. The vision statement should not be so specific that it is time limited. It should be a goal that is attainable throughout the life of the business.

7. See the following example of one inclusive child-care program's vision statement.

> **Vision Statement for ABC Child Development Center**
>
> ABC Child Development Center focuses on serving all children in a play-based environment to benefit the whole development of the child. Our goal is to partner with the family to provide children with a diverse learning experience for children with and without disabilities.

The administration and staff should review the vision statement to see if it is representative of everyone who works with the child-care program and to affirm that it sets realistic goals. The vision statement should shape all major business decisions moving forward, so it is important to get an accurate depiction of the vision from everyone involved.

It is also important to use the vision statement in a sincere manner. If, for example, a program says that serving children with disabilities is the top priority, then the policies and program operations should support that. An inclusive child-care program will not dismiss every child who has a repetitive biting record nor require all children to be toilet trained before moving to the three-year-old classroom. The vision statement, the mission statement, and the program's actions must align to demonstrate the sincerity of the values listed.

The vision statement should be accurate for years to come, but remember that it is a living document. If the direction of the business needs to change, then the vision statement should be updated to match. Goals are not concrete, and the business may need to change at some point to stay operational or relevant. The administration needs to periodically re-evaluate the vision statement to see if it is still reflective of the child-care program and the desired objectives.

CREATING A MISSION STATEMENT

Although a vision statement must be short and concise, a mission statement allows for more elaboration. The mission statement addresses how the school will operate its day-to-day functions and what types of decisions need to be made to align with the mission. The operations of the child-care program to consider can include:

- For-profit or nonprofit status
- Tuition and scholarships
- Staffing priorities
- Professional development
- Enrollment and accepting new students
- Curriculum
- Family involvement
- Community involvement

An inclusive child-care program may include content on accepting children with and without disabilities, using curriculum with a universal design for learning approach (see pages 6-7 for more information), and partnering with families to help children be as successful as possible. There may also be priorities for hiring staff members with experience working with children who have different ability levels and placing a high level of importance on continuing to advance the training of current staff members.

The mission statement will include several sections:

- Name of the child-care program
- Values that are most important to the child-care program, which will guide decisions in the future
- Long-term goals for the child-care program with a measurable timeline for when the center wants to achieve these goals, to gauge whether the program is progressing toward its goals
- Description of what makes the child-care program different from other programs that may be similar in structure—the one or two characteristics that help the program stand out against the competition to help it fully establish an identity. For example: Is this program inclusive? Does it offer pediatric therapy? Is it employee-

based child care? Does the program offer scholarships to community members who can't afford care on their own? Is the program faith-based?

Mission Statement for ABC Child Development Center

At ABC Child Development Center, we believe in providing a developmentally appropriate early childhood education for all young children to help develop the whole child. Our key priorities include:

- Inclusive education
- Lower adult-to-child ratios
- Play-based education
- Focused professional development for our staff
- Curriculum that benefits the whole child
- Family involvement
- Community engagement

We believe that all children need access to high-quality care and education beginning at birth. We also believe that children with disabilities, children exposed to trauma, and children born with special health-care needs will require accommodations and additional supports to be successful in the classroom setting. We strive to partner with the child's entire support team (parents or guardians, special-education teachers, therapists, and medical professionals) to make sure that all children can receive the best possible care and be as prepared as possible to start kindergarten.

We believe that children receive higher-quality care and education when there are fewer children per adult in the classroom setting. This is why we operate at the adult-to-children ratios established by the National Association for the Education of Young Children. We also believe that individual interactions between a child and adult have the greatest effect on individualized learning, and those interactions can only happen when each adult is responsible for a smaller number of children.

We believe that young children learn best through unstructured play instead of a series of structured activities. This means that the classroom environment should be tailored to the learning and development needs of the children, and all children can explore and experiment in the classroom environment. We believe that the teaching staff are in the classroom to guide this learning process and ask the children questions to further their learning.

We believe that our teachers need specialized training on how to support children with disabilities, mental-health needs, and exposure to trauma. We believe that young teachers need mentors and that all teachers need well-thought-out professional-development plans to learn new skills. We also believe that our administrators are resources for our educators and that administrators should be present in the classrooms to observe and guide our teaching staff.

We believe in supporting every area of the child's development, including motor skills (large motor and fine motor), speech and language skills, cognitive skills, social and emotional skills, independence skills, hygiene skills, and pre-academic skills. We believe in using developmental assessments in the classroom to see which skills the children are mastering and which skills the children need more time to master. We believe in using a variety of activities and materials to teach these skills instead of having children sit at desks to complete work.

We believe that families are the experts on their own children. We believe that teaching staff need to speak with the family first when trying to learn new information about the children. We also believe that constant communication with the family will help develop consistency between the home and school environment.

We believe in using the community as a resource when educating young children. We strive to collaborate with the community, particularly the public school system, to structure curriculum for the children in our care. We believe in creating a diverse system of learning in our child-care program, and we strive to use the resources available in the community to offer the children a well-rounded education.

Starting the Writing Process for the Mission Statement

Like the vision statement, the mission statement should use concise vocabulary that helps different individuals read the same document and understand the same information. It also needs to be realistic. While the vision statement provides the ideal scenario, the mission statement takes a more operational viewpoint. The policies and operations should align with and support the ideals of the vision statement to make them a reality.

For example, if the mission statement talks about supporting the community by offering a scholarship program for qualifying families, then the program must have a way to fund that program instead of simply dreaming. If the program isn't feasible at the time the mission statement is written, then the statement may prioritize community involvement with a five- or ten-year goal for donations to support a designated number of scholarships per year. Similarly, if the mission statement prioritizes teacher education to train staff to work with children with disabilities but the budget does not support paying salaries that are competitive for staff members with college degrees, then that goal may not yet be realistic.

Finally, the mission statement should have some measurable goals. All program stakeholders—administrators, teachers, parents and guardians, and community members—should be involved in brainstorming these goals. The dates and timelines for the goals should be concrete enough that the administration can assess its progress annually and figure out if operational changes need to be made to keep the program on course. Specific dates don't have to be offered, but annual guidelines can be helpful. Writing long-term goals further than five or ten years away often causes teachers and administrators to feel that the goals are distant so they do not have to work on them in the present. A mission statement should apply to everyone working at the child-care program, and they should understand that the program goals apply to them.

Bringing together a diverse group of people can offer a lot of feedback. If the teachers have the opportunity to give input on how the program operates, they are more likely to support program changes. The administrators and teachers participate in the program all day, yet the community also has a vested interest in the program's success. Reliable child care supports the employees of many of the businesses in the community, so business leaders may want to express the needs of the community as a whole. Parents and guardians are the primary consumers of the child-care program, so they can share information and ideas on how the program can best support them. For example, they can offer suggestions on the business hours needed, how much they can afford to pay, and what they want for their children. Everyone's voices should be represented in the brainstorming discussion. Then, the administration can review the suggestions to determine what the program is realistically capable of doing.

Program Values

The program values will affect individuals inside and outside the company. It is important to select only a few and commit to those, instead of listing every value that the administration thinks consumers and donors may appreciate. The listed values are going to attract potential staff members to the organization, and, ultimately, not following through will affect staff morale because they won't feel that the company is true to its purpose.

Start by looking at the purpose of the program. What does the child-care program want to do? Obviously, the people in the program want to care for children with and without disabilities in a group setting when their families are not present, but where does it go from there? Does the program want to meet the state's minimum standards, or does it have a goal to meet best practice standards? Is there a certain group of children within the disability community that the program wishes to serve? Is the program focusing on community members, or is there a sub-group of families who are the primary audience for the program? For example, this could be low-income families, families who share the same religious beliefs, families with children who have disabilities, or families from a certain culture. It could be families who all work for the same company or families who work unusual hours and need child care at nontraditional times. Whatever the program's purpose, that information should lead off the core values.

Next, the administration needs to consider the values that make the program different from others with a similar purpose. If the program opens enrollment to children with disabilities, for example, then how does the program support the children and families differently? What values does the program demonstrate with its purpose? Also, what about those values is a sacrifice? If the program is high quality, does it purposefully lower its adult-to-child ratios to obtain that high quality, even though the program can't make as much money that way? If the program supports children with disabilities, does it hire more staff to make sure that teachers get breaks and children have an extra adult when they need one? If the program serves children and families with low incomes, then how does it ensure its continued ability to pay its bills and provide quality care to the children? Identifying those sacrifices can help programs see the core values they are acting out daily. In the child-care industry, some of the core values that may be part of a mission statement include:

- Developmentally appropriate practice
- Developing attached relationships between teachers and students
- Serving children with and without disabilities
- Making sure that all children have access to child care, regardless of family income
- Following the interests of the child to plan curriculum
- Using a whole-child curriculum to help children develop in each area of growth
- Collaboration with families
- Collaboration with the public and private school systems
- Community partnerships, to make sure families in the community have child-care access so family members can go to work and support their families financially
- Kindergarten readiness

- Lifelong learning for child-care teachers and staff
- Creating a healthy community with nutritious food and active children
- Administrators who train and support the program teaching staff

These are all admirable values, but it is challenging for a child-care program to prioritize and maintain all of them. Programs must focus on what aligns with the vision statement and is the most important to the program and the families enrolled.

Long-Term Goals

An effective, guiding mission statement must contain some long-term goals that give the child-care program a path forward. These decisions lay the foundation for the next five to ten years of the business, based on the current vision. So much can happen in a five-year period that the planning group needs to have a focused process on how to write these goals. The initial brainstorming session should begin with deciding where the administration wants the program to be in five years. Visualizing the future can show the administrators the goal from which the program should work backward and determine what changes will need to be made to achieve that goal.

Again, this requires the administration to be realistic in deciding how much change a program is really capable of and in identifying aspects of the program that do not need to change. Once there are specific ideas for future changes, then the administration needs to prioritize those changes and determine which ones to address first. The number of goals a program is able to select depends on how "long-term" those goals are. Two to three goals is usually the maximum that a program can focus on at any given time. Once a program selects those two to three goals, then they need to break down the steps for how to address them. For a sample, we will use an example program that has selected the following two goals:

- Each classroom in the child-care program will be inclusive.
- Teaching staff will be trained and supported to work with a diverse group of children.

Breaking down the long-term goals into smaller steps or into short-term goals can assist with creating more concrete details. If the program wants to make sure that teachers are trained and supported to work with a diverse group of students, then what steps will that involve?

- Lead teachers may need to have a degree in the field of early childhood education.

- All teaching staff may need to focus their annual professional-development hours on learning about disabilities, diverse cultures, and medical needs of students.

- The program director may need to assess each staff member's strengths and weaknesses in the classroom to determine which specific trainings are needed.

- The program director may need to offer lead teachers planning time to make sure that lesson plans meet the needs of all the children in the classroom.

- The program director may need to assist teachers with parent-teacher conferences, as needed so that families know that teachers have the support of the program administration.

These five smaller goals make the long-term goal seem more achievable. They can also help the administrator determine which goals can happen faster than others. Having the administrator assist with parent-teacher conferences as needed would be a short-term goal. That would only be a scheduling change. However, lead teachers having a college degree would be a longer-term project, because current staff members may not have a degree.

The key to reaching a long-term goal, such as making sure that lead teachers have early childhood degrees, is to make it a measurable and realistic goal. If only 50 percent of the current lead teachers have college degrees, then it would be appropriate to look at a five-year plan for all lead teachers to earn a degree. Make the goal measurable. For example, establish a specific number, such as 100 percent of the lead teachers will have a college degree in a field related to early childhood education. And because education is expensive, the program would need to find a way to make the process realistic. For current employees without a degree, the school might use their state's early childhood scholarship program to help them attain that education. Then, current staff members would not have to worry about losing their jobs. New hires would be required to have already earned a degree. The program director could track the progress over time for the percentage of lead teachers with a completed degree and the progress of the teachers who are working toward a degree. Overall, the long-term goal would be achievable and would contribute to the larger goal of educated and supported teachers.

Evaluating a Timeline

Setting the timelines for the goals is important, but it is also important that the timelines remain accurate and relevant to the program. Establish regular intervals at which time the administration can review the progress on the long-term goals shared in the mission statement and whether those goals need to be adapted. Staff should also be updated on goal performance so that they can see the path of the program. If, for example, the administrative board reviews the program goals each quarter, then the program director may give an annual update to the staff to show the direction that the program is heading and how the staff can help the program to advance.

The administration and the teaching staff must work together for the mission statement to be as effective as possible. For example, the first goal of the mission statement may be to focus on serving children with and without disabilities in an inclusive child-care environment, but the mission statement may also set a goal to support children in the community who cannot afford inclusive child care. In that case, the administration may develop a measurable timeline regarding when the scholarship program may realistically begin. So, perhaps the scholarship program is a five-year goal to give the program time to accumulate donations and fund the project.

A vision statement and mission statement guide the decision-making process of the child-care program. If serving children with disabilities is at the heart of that vision and mission, then that goal will influence all further decisions. These statements also help others understand the values of the program. New ideas for goals that are proposed from time to time will need to be evaluated in light of the existing goals and values. For example, if parents suggest expanding the child-care program to add a science, technology, engineering, and mathematics (STEM) lab for the children, that is an excellent goal. However, it isn't the driving vision and mission of an inclusive child-care program. The administration may decide to decline that request and find a project that better aligns with the core values of the organization.

The Vision of a Director

Shirley is the director of a mixed-delivery private preschool program in the southern United States that uses an inclusive child-care model. The program partners with the local public school system, so it serves children who attend for free because they are enrolled in public school preschool. The program also serves children whose families pay tuition because they are enrolled through the private child-care program. Shirley has worked in the field of early childhood education for more than twenty-five years, and during the majority of that time she has worked with young children with disabilities.

I have an opportunity that many child-care directors do not have: running a child-care program that specializes in working with children who have significant disabilities. My program started off working with children with significant visual disabilities, blind or near blind. Our mission is empowering families by providing educational excellence to young children with visual impairments to help them build a strong foundation for reaching their highest potential. We have a mixed enrollment of children so that the children with disabilities have same-age peers who are typically developing and can set a positive example for our children with disabilities. The breakdown of our enrollment for children with and without disabilities depends on how many children the public school system sends us each year. Usually, at least half of the children enrolled in our program have a diagnosed disability, and the vast majority of those children have visual impairments.

When other program directors and owners ask me about being the director of an inclusive child-care program, I have so many reasons for why this work is important. First, I just feel like it is the right thing to do. These are extremely vulnerable children, and their families are confused, scared, and looking for answers. We need to be there to help them. Second, we are creating a community of children who care about others. We hear stories about how the sighted peers in our program have increased their compassion and understanding, and I can tell you that it is true. All my grandchildren went through this program. They were in the classroom with a variety of children, and it changed their lives. My rambunctious four-year-old grandson told me, "I have some friends that don't talk. They just think a lot." He never heard his friends' voices, but he knew that they had their own perspectives. By being inclusive, you aren't taking away a thing from the typically developing children, but you are giving to everyone in the program.

People often ask how our program is different. The biggest differences between our program and other child-care programs are that we have trained special-education teachers who work with our students and we have low adult-to-child ratios so that even our typically developing students receive an individualized education.

We are blessed to partner with our local school district in a mixed-delivery format. This means that we receive a significant stipend from the public school system to help support the children in our program. It also means that we are responsible for completing all the requirements of the IDEA, because we receive those funds. Although our mission focuses on working with children with visual impairments, the public school contract means that we also serve preschoolers who use wheelchairs or children who require a feeding tube. Our classroom structure and individualized environment lends itself to supporting all children with disabilities.

Our screening processes for new students typically focus on finding children with visual impairments who need a specialized education. We look for characteristics that are typical for young children (especially in the toddler and young preschool years) that indicate visual impairments. This can include traits such as lack of eye contact or not reaching for toys. Those are also some of the early signs of autism spectrum disorder (ASD), so we do see some instances in which children that we initially thought might have visual impairments end up with a diagnosis of ASD instead.

My teaching staff is absolutely amazing. My lead teachers have dual certifications in interdisciplinary early childhood education (IECE) and in special education with a vision impaired endorsement. The IECE certificate gives the teachers a broad background to interact with all the children of different ability levels, but their background in vision is what makes our program stand out. When we have children with medical complications who need interventions such a gastronomy tube (G-tube), then the local school system will come to train the teachers on how to care for the children, depending on how complicated the medical procedures are. My teachers do tube feedings and administer emergency medications such as EpiPens, seizure medications, and insulin injections. We have at least two teachers in each classroom who are certified for G-tube feedings. If a child's medical needs are more complex, then we may have to work with the family to get a nurse to stop by and offer the treatment.

When I look for additional trainings for my teaching staff, I look for trainings that could be associated with the causes of vision loss. Right now, for example, we focus on trainings such as pediatric abusive head trauma, lead poisoning, and malnutrition. Of course, by the time we meet the child, he or she is already experiencing vision loss, but I think it is important for the teachers to understand the whole process. We also do a lot of trainings related to sensory learning. Many children with vision loss seek other sensory experiences, and we want to make sure that those are offered in the classroom to help them take in as much information as possible. For our general disability population, the teachers also take classroom-management trainings and trainings on writing IEPs.

The therapists who work with the children in our preschool program come through the local school system, so again, our partnership with the school district offers a lot of services that support our students. Our lead classroom teachers are considered the visual-impairment specialists, but all the other specialists come from the school district. The school system will send speech pathologists, occupational therapists, or physical therapists. Occasionally, we have students who are diagnosed with two sensory disabilities, and we eventually recommend them to the Deaf-Blind Project in our area. However, they might have a hearing-impairment specialist see them at our program as they determine the significance of the disability. Since all children in the public school system with an IEP must be re-evaluated at least every three years, we also collaborate with the public school system's diagnostician. She may be in the classroom conducting observations, or we may provide her with some outside space so that she and the child can work together. Our building also houses early intervention services for children under the age of three, so there is support space that can be used by any of the therapists who need one-on-one time with a child.

With a nationwide staffing crisis, we have had a difficult time keeping some of our assistant teachers and substitutes, but our lead teachers have been consistent and are dedicated to the mission. When we have open assistant positions, that means that the children with visual impairments don't have someone trying to engage them in the classroom and they are sitting alone. That can't happen, so we push on and find a way to get the assistant teachers that we need. We do occasionally lose staff to the public school system; usually when that happens, those teachers have decided to work with older children. Working with three- and four-year-olds with significant disabilities is a very challenging job, and it takes a specific personality and determination to fill that role. If someone would rather work with the older students, then we would rather find someone whose passion is working with our preschoolers.

The special-education endorsement in visual impairments is not common. Since we need teachers who have that background, we will offer to fund the teacher's education for the master's degree in visual impairments. The teacher's contract will specify that we will pay for the education, and then they will work for us for five years after the degree is complete. If the teacher decides to leave before then, they can pay us back the prorated cost that is remaining. This program makes sure that we can find the specialized teachers that we need, and we don't have to place an unqualified teacher in the classroom. It also increases the teachers' knowledge so that more educators know how to support a wide range of students.

Children who come to us from some of the smaller surrounding communities have often struggled significantly in their previous child-care settings. Their public school systems may have offered them two days or three days of preschool per week, and those may have only been half days. Without constant support, those children have just not progressed the same way that the children in our full-day program do. The families will come to us and tell us that their children sat alone in a corner of the classroom, and no one spoke to them. Children with visual impairments may be overwhelmed by lots of colors and activity in the classroom, so they turn their heads away from all the stimulation. When the teachers in those classrooms don't know how to support them and draw them out, then the children sit isolated in the corner of the room with no interactions and no progress.

Preschoolers who enroll through our program, instead of through the public school system, receive their therapies with our team members. Our preschool teachers are considered the visual-impairment specialists, but the children can receive other support services through our center. We have two team members who specialize in orientation and mobility for children with visual impairments. We also have an early interventionist who works in our building for children under the age of three. Some of those specialists can support the privately enrolled students, and their services can be paid for in cash by the family or privately billed through the family's health insurance.

Children who come to us from school districts that we don't have formal contracts with will utilize multiple services in our building along with the preschool. Some areas of our state have almost no resources outside of the public school system, so it isn't unusual for families to drive quite a distance to bring their children to our program. Then, of course, there are more families on the waiting list who would love to drive to our county, but they are on the waiting list for some time before we can support them.

Our program is lucky that we have never had a waitlist for the children who live in our service area. A full-time student at our program comes five days a week, but not all children want to come that much. We have children who come two days, three days, or four days a week instead. If the child is enrolled through the local school district, then we are contractually obligated to enroll them for five days a week. When a family contacts us and wants to get their child in, we find a way to enroll them even if they have to wait for a five-day-per-week spot. We will start them off with two to three days, and as enrollment allows, we will eventually move them up to five days.

Changing daily enrollment can definitely alter staffing somewhat. We never have fewer than three teachers in the classroom at one time. We never come close to the maximum state ratios, so that is not an issue. If we have a day that has more students, then we may add a floater or substitute to a classroom to make it easier for the teachers to support all of the children. Plus, depending on the day, we may have multiple therapists in the classroom who are working with children and giving them individual attention.

Our preschool program is a nonexpulsion program due to our partnership with the public school system. Because our classroom ratios are so low, we typically develop strong relationships with the families so expulsion is not typically an issue. Also, our families referred to the school through the public school system do not have to pay tuition; they are receiving a private school education for a public school cost. Since tuition payments are not a problem, then we don't have to deal with expulsion of students with disabilities due to lack of payment. The families who enroll through the tuition program do not want to endanger their spot in the preschool, so we rarely have families who miss payments. We do occasionally have an issue in which children are initially admitted to the program because we think they have vision impairments but they are later diagnosed as being on the autism spectrum. In those cases, we don't expel the family, but we do tell them that we might not be the best educational setting for their child. We help them find an educational program that is better suited for children with autism, and we let them complete the whole school year before that transition occurs.

Although we spend a lot of time providing additional services for our children with disabilities, it is obvious that their typically developing peers are also excelling in the classroom. We often reach out to families after they graduate from our program to see how the child is transitioning into kindergarten. Parents tell us success stories about how their typically developing child is not only doing well but is excelling in the new environment. The children are prepared academically to enter school, but that is not the point on which parents focus. Most families are thrilled with the compassion that their children have developed by being in such a diverse classroom setting. Teachers in their new schools will comment that the children who graduated from our program are more compassionate to students who are different than others.

Our program is designed to work with the whole family. We have an open-door policy so parents can come and observe in the classroom anytime they want. One definite difference of serving children with vision impairments is that parents can observe without the children seeing them. Parents can see what the typical classroom setting looks like on any given day, and the child won't alter their behavior for the parent's benefit. Prior to the COVID-19 pandemic, we had a monthly parent event on-site, but now many of those events have shifted online, which enables more parents to attend.

We try to do different types of family education throughout the year, and our most popular class is always about the transition out of our program into the public school setting. Families are always nervous to leave our small community, so that event comes with lots of participation and lots of questions. We also have an annual event on estate planning to care for a child after the parents are gone. And every November we hold a family retreat. The children do a camp, and the parents get a retreat to focus on self-care. Many of these families have never had a babysitter because no one knows how to care for the child. The program partners with a hotel to fund a weekend away, and approximately twenty-five families participate each year.

Families are often interested in learning Braille, but that is not necessarily the content that they need to know when their child is in preschool. We give the family some basic training with simple words and help them put labels up in the home. Most children with visual impairments don't learn in the same path that typically developing children do, so a preschool child doesn't necessarily need to begin learning words like an older child would. Of course, the parents may only know the typical path of development, and they get nervous that their children are not learning everything that they need to learn. Eventually, the children will learn Braille, but that is more of a focus in elementary school and middle school. I think parents focus on it so much because it is a concrete step that they can take and understand. It is hard for them to see a nonlinear path that they have never had to go down themselves.

Staffing is by far our biggest cost, but we have never been in danger of not being able to pay for the staff we need. We have always had generous donors, and because our mission statement is so defined and specific, it attracts some donors who may be looking to support a group of children and families who have been overlooked. With donations, the school system contract, tuition, and therapy billing, we have always been able to meet the needs of our budget.

The donations are wonderful, but we also rely heavily on grants and foundations to help with the cost of general operations. In the past, we had this philosophy that if a staff member found a grant that he or she liked, then they needed to write it. Now, we have become much more intentional to maintain our funding. We have a full-time grant writer on staff. The job not only includes searching for and writing new grants, but also collecting data for the grants that are open so that we can maintain those sources of funding. The idea of adding an entire paid position for grant writing seemed overwhelming when we first introduced it. Now, when we see how much that full-time position can yield, the annual salary expense seems minimal. The children with disabilities in an inclusive setting are learning how to advocate for themselves. They are learning how to be a part of a world with lots of different people. They are learning how to get the teacher's attention and make sure their needs are met. In classrooms where every child has a significant disability, you often don't see children developing that type of independence because adults do everything for the children. In inclusive classrooms, we challenge the children to be mobile instead of carrying them where they want to go, and their peers model walking to different parts of the classroom. Our students need to motivate themselves to be a part of a society that may not stop and listen to them. An inclusive setting teaches these children how to advocate, and they have supportive teachers and peers who are cheering them on as they do. There is no reason why child-care programs should not use this type of model.

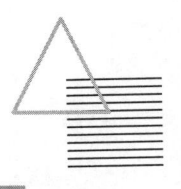

CHAPTER 4

Starting the Transition

Once your child-care program decides to shift its focus and become an inclusive learning environment, you will most certainly need to make changes. But how do you even know what changes to make? Where do you begin? This chapter will help you start the transition by taking it step by step, including:

- conducting a self-assessment,
- establishing goals, and
- creating a transition plan.

CONDUCTING A SELF-ASSESSMENT

It can be overwhelming to sit down and make a list of items to address as you move toward creating an inclusive program. For example, there is staff education to think about and there are policy changes to consider. However, you may find that some of your program operations may already be in line with an inclusive child-care program. Before making any major changes, conduct a full self-assessment to see which areas of the program already support an inclusive environment and which aspects need to be changed.

A quality self-assessment looks at each aspect of the child-care program from curriculum to family engagement to administrative practices. Many accreditation programs, such as that of the National Association for the Education of Young Children (NAEYC), have created a list of each program area to assess during the accreditation process. You can also use this type of comprehensive list to assess which areas of your program need to be updated to provide services to children of all ability levels. NAEYC uses ten standards of quality to mark the different areas of program development. Those standards incorporate many of the same markers that need to be present in an inclusive environment. (See the appendix for a sample self-assessment.)

The major goal of a self-assessment is not to achieve a specific score but to see the areas in which the program needs improvement. Due to the amount of time and cost associated with the changes, you might not want to change certain areas or might want to implement changes over time in phases. Ultimately, the goal is to identify the needs and create a plan for how to implement the changes.

ESTABLISHING GOALS

Once your management team has identified the needs through a self-assessment, the next step is to articulate one or more goals. The goal could be as broad as identifying the standard area that needs improvement, such as Standard 10: Leadership and Management (see page 126). Under this one heading, your program may need to revise the mission statement, rewrite center policies, and update staff handbooks. Broader goals will take longer to accomplish since they can have many specific parts. A smaller goal, such as revising the program mission statement, can still take time. However, it will have a more concrete completion since it is identified as one specific task.

Let's say a center set the goals to give all teachers weekly planning time and to offer additional staffing support to classrooms in which a child has extremely challenging behaviors. These goals would require the center to re-evaluate the staffing schedule to provide a teacher in the classroom while the lead teacher is planning and to find support staff to supplement a classroom that needs an assistant teacher due to challenging behaviors. Both goals will require extra funding to cover the additional paid staff time.

As the list of goals grows, consider the timeline for accomplishing these tasks and setting a realistic expectation for completion. If a center is completely updating all of the management tasks to align with an inclusive philosophy, that may be the first phase of the plan and may take six months to a year to change and implement new practices. (See "Creating a Transition Plan" on pages 54–56).

Using the NAEYC standards as guideposts allows the program to look at all areas of operation, but these standards don't operate independently. They naturally overlap, so changing program policy also affects staff training and family partnerships. This means you'll need to include staff and keep families apprised of the changes. Otherwise, management may implement new policies, but if no one is following through on making sure the policies are being implemented by staff and parents, the policies are essentially useless. Each child-care program will want to share their individualized reasons for this transition with their staff members and enrolled families, but some of the key reasons that many programs choose to transition to an inclusive child-care program may include the following:

- Currently, children are enrolled in each classroom who need more individualized curriculum to be as successful as possible.

- Many children have come to the child-care program after having negative experiences at other programs, and the administration wants to make sure that each child receives necessary supports such as developmental assessments and partnerships with local pediatric therapy programs.

- A partnership with the local public school district will offer supports to children with and without disabilities, as well as specialized training for teachers.

- All changes must be a team approach with management, staff, and families. When a program changes its operations significantly, get feedback from staff and families in the brainstorming process and as implementation takes place. This may mean that the program administrator selects staff and parent leaders to help create new program goals and timelines. Including staff and families means that they will be more invested in the changes because they had a voice in the creation process. They will also be able to encourage others to participate in the program's new mission.

CREATING A TRANSITION PLAN

If your program self-assessment indicates that you need to make significant changes, it may be overwhelming to make them all at once. In that case, start off by making a timeline of when policies need to change. It can be confusing for staff and families if policies change frequently. It may be best to group changes into two to three tiers and group similar changes together. It can also be helpful for staff and families to know the long-term timeline for changes. This information can be shared at the parent meeting to keep everyone informed. For example, tier one changes may be updating internal policies on how to support children with disabilities. Tier two polices may be updating enrollment procedures and opening up the facility to new and diverse families.

Sample Transition Plan for ABC Child Care

1. Offer priority enrollment on the waitlist for children with disabilities at the same level as the priority offered to children who have a sibling already enrolled. Implement in the next three months.

2. Change communication on the program website to indicate that the center serves children with and without disabilities. Implement in the next three months.

3. Train each teacher on trauma-informed care and classroom management for children with disabilities. Start with lead teachers. Implement in the next six months.

4. Contract with a local pediatric occupational therapist to do observations in each classroom and offer feedback to teachers on classroom-management strategies that can support children with and without disabilities. Implement in the next twelve months.

Sample of Transition Plan for Next-Door-Neighbor Child Care

1. Train all teachers on using a developmental assessment tool. Implement within the next two months.

2. Allow teachers planning time to begin using the assessment tool and to feel comfortable with the observation and scoring process. Implement in the next four months.

3. Schedule a parent education night to share information with families on the new developmental assessment and how it will be used in the classroom. Implement in the next six months.

4. Begin scheduling parent-teacher conferences twice per school year during which teachers share the results of the child's developmental assessments with family members. Implement during the following school year.

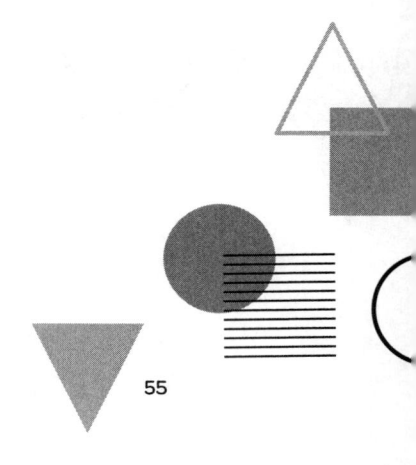

When child-care programs sit down and just make a list of areas to improve upon, it can be difficult to review each area of program administration and make a comprehensive list. The self-assessment helps programs identify all the different considerations for running a high-quality program and consider how to narrow down the larger areas that need more support. If all the weaknesses are under one specific standard, then it may be easier to prioritize the area. If weaknesses are scattered across multiple standards, then priorities may be determined by other factors, such as the cost of implementation. However the priorities are determined, it is always important for the program to take on a reasonable number of goals within a realistic timeline.

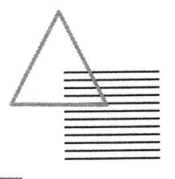

CHAPTER 5

Setting New Policies

To develop an inclusive child-care program, changes usually begin with the policies on how the program is administered or how the program supports all students. The areas in which policies most often require adjustments include:

- Enrollment
- Cost
- Challenging behaviors (including biting and aggression)
- Suspension and expulsion
- Program visitors
- Confidentiality
- Classroom observations

The majority of this chapter will discuss how you might adjust your policies in these particular areas to reflect an inclusive program. The remainder of this chapter delves into revising your program's handbooks. Child-care programs typically have two sets of policies: one for families and one for staff members. Transitioning to an inclusive child-care program will affect policies in both handbooks. Family handbooks usually describe enrollment, billing, family expectations, children's behavior expectations, and classroom procedures. Staff handbooks focus on job descriptions and expectations for staff behavior. Staff handbooks may also be adapted to support employees with disabilities. Depending on what decisions are made by your administration, staff members with disabilities may need additional time off for doctor visits, paid leave, upgrades to facilities like handicap-accessible entrances to the building, or reading assistance during staff training. Child-care programs can set a strong example by supporting both employees and students with disabilities to show that a fully inclusive environment is possible.

ENROLLMENT

All child-care programs need some type of procedure for enrollment. In an inclusive child-care program, it's important that those policies are inclusive to all families. When a program begins to serve children with many different abilities, word gets out and families begin filling out applications for their children. Your program administration must determine how they will serve both typically developing children and children with special needs. If your program continues to enroll children on a first-come, first-served basis, then the center initially may change its policies but not its clientele. Eventually, the majority of the applicants may have special needs. Keep in mind that it can be overwhelming for a teacher to have a classroom full of children with developmental delays, with no typically developing students to model appropriate behaviors. There should be a balance to help make the classroom environment more manageable.

Some centers prefer to have two separate enrollment lists, one for typically developing students and one for children with special needs, which allows the program to select a manageable caseload of needs within each classroom. If your program decides to use this model, you'll need to determine how many slots are reserved in each classroom for typically developing children and for children with special needs. One thing to consider with this model is that children under the age of five may have not been screened for developmental delays. It is possible that you may be enrolling children who have disabilities that have not yet been identified. Many toddlers and preschool-age children are screened for delays in their early childhood programs, and a referral is then made for additional evaluation. This means that a center with two separate waitlists may end up with a classroom that has more needs than anticipated.

Other programs choose to do a small "interview" with all potential students who want to enroll in the program. This can be incorporated into a tour for the adults in the family and can create an opportunity for the classroom teachers to see how the child interacts with same-age peers. A short tour of the facility is not enough time for the teachers to learn everything about a child, especially since viewing a new program can be a novel experience for the child, but it may allow the teachers to identify some red flags. The idea behind this screening method is not to deny a child with special needs access to a classroom, but to determine whether the child would be a good fit for a particular classroom. If the classroom already has children with some challenging behaviors and the child has a high level of needs, then perhaps another classroom would be a better fit. A child with more independence may fit better into the current opening.

However your management team chooses to enroll new students, be sure to include that information in the family handbook.

COST

Transitioning to an inclusive child-care program can come with additional costs. Facility adaptations and new materials incur a one-time cost, but the ongoing cost increases are the additional staffing that may be required to support children with special needs. Children with disabilities may need additional support in the classroom, which usually means that adult-to-child ratios have to be lower than if the students were all typically developing. Your child-care program must determine where the funding for the additional staffing will come from and how much of those funds will be collected in tuition increases.

It is challenging to make a large tuition increase at one time, particularly when families have multiple children enrolled in the program at once. As a rule, child-care programs prefer to make small, incremental increases each year that do not overwhelm the families instead of a large jump all at once. These incremental increases usually account for inflation of the prices of food and materials and for small raises for staff members. A program that plans to add staff will often create a larger rate increase, so the administration will need to map out how to implement the new increases.

Some child-care programs may look for outside funding (such as grants or a donor) to ease families into a series of small rate increases. Other programs may look at their own rates compared to those in the local child-care market to determine how high they can raise the program rates while still being competitive.

Adding additional staff members and reducing adult-to-child ratios is a benefit to the program that affects every student enrolled. Most families can see the benefit of increasing the rates in order to provide higher-quality care; however, rate increases are still a burden. Child care is often one of the family's greatest expenses. It is always possible that a rate increase may encourage a family to choose a new child-care program, but that can be said in any child-care program. If your center increases rates beyond the typical annual increments, consider hosting a meeting to explain to families why the rates are increasing. If your program truly is changing the direction of its mission, make sure all the families you serve understand those changes and the financial impact of those changes.

Some child-care programs choose to grandfather in families that are currently attending the program at a lower rate than what newly enrolling families will pay. This can appease the families who are already enrolled, but it can be hard to justify to new families why they have to pay more for the same service. It is easier to explain why a slot in the infant room costs more than a slot in the preschool classroom based on the additional staffing needed for infants. It is harder to explain why two children in the same classroom are charged two separate rates.

CHALLENGING BEHAVIORS: BITING AND AGGRESSION

All early child-care educators encounter children's challenging behaviors from time to time. As small businesses, early childhood centers have to balance the needs of all the children enrolled with the safety of children and teachers in the classroom when crafting their policies for handling challenging behaviors. Yet, programs must not jump to suspension or expulsion at the first sign of challenging behaviors. You can eliminate many negative behaviors—including biting and aggression—with professional guidance and an understanding of why the behavior occurs.

Because toddlers have limited language skills as a way to communicate, biting is developmentally typical for them. Despite this, families can have strong reactions when their child is bitten by a classmate (NAEYC, 2023). Since so many families have an emotional response when a child in the classroom begins to bite others, many child-care programs have developed strong policies on how to handle a child who repeatedly bites. Some centers may send a child home for the remainder of the school day once the child bites two or three times in one day. Other centers have developed a point system that suspends or expels children once they accumulate a certain number of points. As a small business, a center can create policies that eliminate the number of children in the program who may bite; however, this policy may indirectly target children with disabilities.

Children with speech delays, social delays, or sensory processing dysfunction may bite more often than a typically developing child (NAEYC, 2023). A child who cannot verbally communicate with her classmates may bite to tell them to stop. A child who is alarmed by too much sensory information at one time may bite another child to tell the child to give him more space. Children who crave more sensory information may bite as a method of exploring the environment around them. A child who has delayed social skills may bite another child in a misguided attempt to communicate. Suspending these children or expelling them from the child-care program can eliminate many children with special needs during the toddler years. Do you recall the foster parents' experience with Amal in the first vignette of the book (see pages 15–25)? The trauma he had previously experienced, his developing vocabulary, and his response to too much stimulation in the classroom made it hard to pinpoint why his biting occurred, but the child-care program worked to reduce the triggers and to help him be more successful.

Instead of initially setting a harsh expulsion policy, inclusive child-care programs can think about other steps that may be able to reduce biting and support children with developmental delays. Once a child exhibits a pattern of biting in the classroom, meet with the family. Establish a method of communication to help the family understand when the biting occurs (such as a daily journal that the teachers use for documentation) and a plan for reducing the biting. Suggest supports such as using specific language to tell the child to stop biting and helping the child use simple sign language to ask classroom peers to stop a negative behavior that may trigger biting. Recommend sensory toys such as vibrating teethers or frozen teething rings that can offer additional sensory input. You can also ask an administrator to observe the class to see when the biting occurs and what happens right before and right after, which can help the teachers determine what triggers the behavior. The parents can offer information about how they handle the behavior in the home or in community settings. That information may help direct the school team to accommodations that will be successful in the classroom.

If the biting continues to be a frequent behavior despite accommodations, then the family may need to seek guidance from a specialist such as a speech pathologist or occupational therapist. Some inclusive centers have been willing to allow a child to continue enrollment as long as the family works with a specialist and receives additional strategies to reduce the behavior. Biting can be the first sign that a child may have a developmental delay, and an evaluation by a specialist can help identify other needs that also require support. All child-care programs want to decrease biting in the classroom, but the center policies need to support families who are dealing with larger developmental problems. Establishing a policy helps parents understand that the child-care program is willing to work with the family, but it also shows the family that they need to be involved in the solution to reduce the behavior.

As with biting, a child exhibiting aggressive behavior in the classroom is always a concern to teachers and administrators, because the child could injure themselves or others (including the staff). At some point in childhood development, almost every child hits or kicks, but a continued pattern of aggression is different from a one-time behavior. When it is obvious that a child is showing a pattern of aggression, ensure that your program has policies in place to handle this behavior, which may include recording the details of the aggressive behaviors—what behavior occurred, when it occurred (time of day and classroom routine), what happened immediately before, and if the behavior consistently occurs with the same child or children. Then, share this information with the parents during a family meeting so that the education team and the family can review the information together to see if a pattern is present. Use the initial meeting with the family to create strategies to help eliminate the behavior in the classroom. For example, if a child continuously hits others during circle time, then perhaps that child needs an alternative setting for circle time. He might be overstimulated sitting in a circle with all of his peers, so allowing him to move around the room while still listening to the teacher could eliminate the aggression. The child's teachers can agree to follow up with the family after making changes in the classroom.

Most child-care programs will attempt the first conference with the family, but if those initial changes do not eliminate the negative behaviors, then many programs will ask the family to find another place for their child. This is typically not done in a spiteful manner, but the center wants to make sure that all the children in the classroom stay safe. Safety is always the top priority, but if your program supports children with special needs, take additional measures to make sure that the child receives the help needed. When a child with special needs is suspended or expelled from a child-care program, it can be much harder on that child than a typically developing child. Many children with special needs have a difficult time with major transitions and struggle to get acquainted with new teachers and peers. It is even more important to get to the root of the problem and help them be successful in the classroom.

As the teacher attempts to implement new techniques discussed in the first family-teacher conference, continued documentation can offer valuable insight into the causes of the behavior. If the child is referred for a developmental assessment or sees a specialist, the teacher's documentation can help the doctors or therapists identify important factors. A partnership with the family also means that the teachers and administrators can review the information and recommendations provided by the child's doctors and therapy team. While not every suggestion from the therapy team or doctor will be possible in a group child-care setting, the therapy team usually can provide some classroom-based interventions that work well. The therapist might also visit the classroom to observe the child in the natural classroom setting or do therapy in the classroom to help coach the teachers. These types of partnerships can be a huge asset to the child-care program, with no cost expectation on the program.

In a truly inclusive program, early childhood professionals do what they can to help children be successful and to partner with families. Suspension and expulsion should always be the last option, and it should really be reserved for instances where safety is the greatest concern. Each program should write the suspension and expulsion policy according to its own needs, but it is important to have the policy in writing so that families know what to expect when problem behaviors occur.

SUSPENSION AND EXPULSION

One of the most challenging decisions that an administrator may have to make is whether or not one particular child needs to leave the program. Because child-care programs are individual small businesses, the suspension and expulsion rate in a birth-to-five program is four times higher than suspension and expulsion rates in kindergarten through twelfth-grade education (Meek and Gilliam, 2016). In addition, the public school system receives a special stream of funds from IDEA that gives extra support to children with disabilities, which can provide additional staffing or resources for children who have behavior challenges. Most birth-to-five programs do not have those supports, so child-care programs may feel that their staffing and resources are not adequate to support children with more significant needs.

Depending on the severity of a child's disabilities, a group care setting may not be appropriate for the child. For example, a child who needs one-on-one care may not be able to attend a group child-care program, because the adult-to-child ratios may not allow the child to have all the time and attention required. Parents must consider the significance of the child's needs before selecting a child-care program. Programs with lower adult-to-child ratios are more likely to accommodate children with greater needs.

It is not solely the family's responsibility to consider whether or not the child is able to be in inclusive child care. Child-care programs must consider how they can support children and families. Some suspension and expulsion procedures are set up to dismiss families simply because the program is inconvenienced. That type of policy can deter enrollment from families with atypically developing children. A child-care program needs to consider what issues would constitute a need for suspension or expulsion, what warnings should be put into place, and what actions would trigger expelling a child or family.

Lack of payment is obviously one of the issues that could mean suspension or expulsion. A small business that is providing a service deserves payment in return so that it can continue to operate and to pay staff. A child-care program's payment policy should explain when payment is due and define consequences if payment is late. If payment is missed for one week, then a late fee may be assessed, but the second week the payment is missed can lead to dismissal. Payment policies can seem cruel, but it may be the difference between a center being able to stay open or closing. If the program does have a small amount of funding that could be used to cover missed payments, then perhaps families could apply for "scholarship funds" to help them through a hardship to avoid expulsion.

Other reasons for suspension or expulsion are typically related to child behavior or parent behavior. Negative parent behavior could include cursing, yelling, or threatening staff members. Of course, all programs hope that this would never occur at their program, but unfortunately, it happens more than anyone would like. Parent behavior can have a negative impact on a child's enrollment at times. If a parent uses inappropriate language or threatening behavior on the school grounds, then it is up to the child-care program to decide if a warning is warranted or whether that parent should be banned from entering the program again. If the parent is banned, then the child would either need another reliable adult to provide transportation to and from school, or the child would need to leave the program.

> **ABC Child Development Center: Suspension and Expulsion Policy**
>
> Suspension and expulsion are only used at ABC Child Development Center under the most dire circumstances.
>
> - If a family has not paid tuition for two weeks and cannot work out a payment plan with the administrative office, the child's enrollment will be suspended until payments are up to date. After two weeks of suspension, the child will be disenrolled from the child-care program.
>
> - If a child is demonstrating continuous aggressive behaviors, and the family will not partner with the child-care program to obtain all the necessary supports that the child needs to be successful, then the child's enrollment will be terminated.

PROGRAM VISITORS

Every child-care program has policies regarding who can visit, as well as how and when non-staff members can come into the building. Children with disabilities suffer higher rates of violence than typically developing children (Fang et al., 2022). Consequently, in an inclusive program, keeping all the children safe is of utmost importance. When transitioning to an inclusive program, you'll need to look at your policies carefully to ensure they can accommodate the needs of families of children with disabilities. Some visitors must have access to the building, but, for the purposes of program security, administrators may want to limit unnecessary visitors. In all programs, parents must be able to access the building, and many families will have other relatives or friends that are also responsible for drop-off and pick-up due to the family's work schedule.

Once your program begins to serve children with disabilities, families may request that their child's occupational therapist, speech pathologist, or other health-care professional be allowed to work with their child in the classroom. As stated earlier, this is a benefit for the child and the program—not only can the private therapists see children in a group setting, where a child's behavior can often change, but the classroom teachers get the opportunity to learn from the therapists. Specialists can teach the early childhood educators techniques that can be used with multiple children in the classroom. Child-care providers do not always receive extensive special-education training, so the therapist can provide on-site training that can help with so many children and different types of disabilities.

Typically, when a therapist works with a child on-site at a child-care program, they will visit the child multiple times. If the therapist makes multiple visits to the program, have a background check on file, which should be available from their agency. Many states' licensing agencies will accept that background check for a visitor. In the event that the state requires the child-care program to file its own background check, then the program can coordinate that with the therapist.

Occasionally, the therapist may wish to pull a child out of the classroom briefly to work one on one. Because the therapist is not an employee of the center, the program may need to obtain a signed release from the family to allow the child to leave the classroom with the therapist, as long as the child and therapist stay in the facility. Another option is for the family to add the therapist's name to the approved pick-up list. When the therapist arrives, they could temporarily sign the child out so they can work together in a private space and then sign the child back in when they return to the classroom. This program would need to share this information with the family before the therapist begins visiting the program. The family would be responsible for sharing the protocols with the therapists.

Every child-care program also will have a list of other professionals who need access to the building, such as facility repair workers, plumbers, electricians, and so on. The administrators may prefer that these professionals only have access to the building after hours so that maintenance staff do not have any interactions with children. However, after-hours repair work can be costly, so some programs ask their consistent maintenance workers to have background checks. This helps the administration feel comfortable with the people who access the building when children are present.

Many child-care programs make the decision to host student observers and practicum teachers. Not only does this benefit the students by helping them complete their observation hours, but it also can have a huge benefit for the child-care program.

Adding a student to the classroom provides an additional adult to assist with caring for the children. Plus, students can bring new ideas to the classroom environment and help experienced teachers learn new teaching techniques. Most states require specific background checks for students who visit a program multiple times, so the administration will need to make sure to follow all state requirements.

It is also important to remember that, even though the background checks have been completed, a student observer is not an employee of the child-care program. Staff members cannot leave children alone with a student teacher. The program may also want to implement additional protocols such as whether a student teacher can change diapers or assist children with more personal activities. Just as a staff member has a job description, it is important for a student observer or student teacher to have a clear understanding of expectations from the center when beginning their observation.

Most child-care programs also have community visitors, because potential families may want a tour of the facility before enrolling their own children. There needs to be some balance on how often visitors interrupt normal classroom schedules, especially if there are children with disabilities enrolled who depend on a consistent schedule or may have atypical anxiety.

A child-care program could consider conducting tours after hours, but then the prospective family would not get to see how the teachers interact with the children. That is usually what the family wants to see the most. A better option may be to have two to three days a week when tours are offered at certain times of day. For example, the transition from lunch to naptime is already challenging, so it would be overwhelming to have a family tour of a classroom during that time of day. The entire naptime is also a poor time to offer a tour, since parents would miss seeing those teacher-child interactions and sleeping children may wake up when visitors enter the room. The best time for a tour is typically between nine and eleven in the morning when the classrooms are active and busy. The administrator may need to avoid touring certain classrooms if particular children are overwhelmed by seeing visitors. That is a request that visiting parents can easily understand.

CONFIDENTIALITY

Information about individual children enrolled in any child-care program should always be confidential. When a child-care program works with children who have medical information and disability information on file, staff may need to access that information for the child's care and education. However, that information must be kept confidential from visitors and other families in the program. FERPA is a federal law that requires educational information to be kept private (see page 32). Although child-care programs are not federal organizations, many receive some type of federal funding. Other child-care programs may specifically partner with the local public school. Private medical information is protected by HIPAA. This privacy law can specifically come into effect in a child-care program when a therapist comes to the center to work with a child.

Regardless of a child-care program's funding streams or partnerships, professionalism dictates that teachers and administrators only share private information about a child with those who care for that child and with the child's family. Key medical information should be posted in a secure location in the classroom where the general public cannot see it, such as on the inside door of a cabinet or in a binder that is stored in a safe location. When children have an official document regarding a disability, such as an IEP created by the public school system, only the teachers who work with that child should review that personal information. Although children younger than five years can have these documents from the public school system and still be enrolled in a private child-care program, many children may not have been through the public school evaluation process yet. Instead, the family may provide information from their pediatrician, diagnostician, or private therapist on the child's medical diagnosis and strategies on how to work with the child in the classroom. Regardless of the source of the diagnosis, handle the documents with care and only share private information with a small group of teachers and administrators. Teaching staff need to review the program confidentiality policies on a regular basis (perhaps annually) and sign off that they agree to follow these policies. In addition, offer training to staff members so that they understand how to maintain confidentiality in the classroom and in casual conversations with peers or families.

Many families are curious about how their children are developing compared to other children in this classroom. This is usually a parent's way of determining whether their child is learning the skills that they are supposed to master. When a parent comes into the classroom and begins to ask questions about other children's development, it is important to keep the confidentiality of the other children in the classroom environment. The teacher does not need to share another child's diagnosis or whether that child is meeting developmental milestones.

If the child-care program has student observers, practicum students, student teachers, or other visitors in and out of the building, they also need to review and agree to the program confidentiality policy.

CLASSROOM OBSERVATIONS

When transitioning to an inclusive environment, the program administrator also needs to consider how families and outside professionals can observe the classroom. Some programs have a closed-circuit camera system that allows families to log in to the classroom from off-site or from specific computers on-site at the facility, allowing them to view how the children behave in the classroom without the family's presence. Many parents feel safer knowing that they can watch their child at any point during the day, and it shows that the child-care program offers a high level of accountability when they are willing to let the family see the classroom at any point in time. Although this can be an attractive option for families, and even a marketing tool, this approach has its disadvantages. For example, if a child in the classroom is struggling with biting, then all the other families can view the classroom video to figure out which child is the biter. Confidentiality can also be an issue when a pediatric therapist is in the classroom to work with a child. Other families viewing the classroom can easily determine which child may have a disability.

Another option for classroom observations is for the program administrator to have access to the closed-circuit camera system in their office. The administrator can invite parents to view the footage when a parent needs to observe without the child being aware. This increases confidentiality but still allows families to view the child's behaviors. It also helps the teachers if they are trying to explain certain behaviors the child is exhibiting so that the family understands what is happening. This type of camera system can also be helpful for administrators to view and assess staff or for the state's licensing and monitoring agency to view classrooms during monitoring visits.

Child-care programs may choose not to use a camera system and just allow families to observe in the classroom. Although this policy encourages parents to feel welcome in the classroom, they may not be able to see their child's typical behavior. When a family member arrives, a child usually wants to show them the entire classroom and favorite toys and to introduce friends, which is wonderful information for the parent to learn about but isn't the child's typical behavior. However observations are conducted, you may still want to include a policy on confidentiality during classroom observations in the family handbook.

STAFF AND FAMILY HANDBOOKS

For the parents, a handbook is a way to communicate expectations and to establish mutual accountability between the families and the child-care program. For staff members, the employee handbook establishes job expectations and responsibilities. Once your program has established its foundational policies for an inclusive child-care setting, you'll need to ensure that families and staff know about these policies. Most well-run child-care programs already have family and staff handbooks; however, in an inclusive child-care program, it's important to weave the theme of serving all children throughout the handbooks, with an emphasis on meeting the medical, emotional, physical, and educational needs of each child. The following sections detail how you might specifically incorporate the needs of children with disabilities throughout your staff and family handbooks.

Mission and Vision

If your child-care program is changing its focus to be inclusive of all children, make sure that the staff and families know and understand the direction that the program is taking. Your mission and vision statements need to be at the front of both the family and staff handbooks because these will be the guiding principles for all decisions moving forward. These statements can include information about what inclusion means to the center and who is included in an inclusive environment (children with disabilities, children who have experienced trauma, children with medical conditions, children who speak different languages, and so on). (See chapter 3 for additional information about vision and mission statements.) It may also be helpful to include information about how an inclusive environment helps children of all ability levels. This may clarify to some parents whether their children are still a good fit for the program and to some potential staff if this is a good fit for them as a work environment.

In the family handbook, some child-care programs may also want to include a brief statement about group child care. Although a child-care program may be inclusive, it is still group care, and children will not be able to receive one-on-one instruction. Most children can thrive in group child care and continue into a group setting for their education from kindergarten through high school. However, the public school system can provide individual aides for children with severe disabilities to make sure they get the individualized care that they need. Private child care does not have the financial ability to provide individualized child care, so children enrolled in the program must be independent enough to share the classroom environment with others.

In your program's staff handbook, emphasize that your child-care program is focusing on supporting children with and without disabilities in an inclusive environment. Staff also need to understand that an inclusive environment will include dealing with some challenging behaviors and unique health conditions. This is not entirely different from a typical child-care program, because children with unique needs attend almost all child-care programs. However, an inclusive child-care program will not dismiss a child from care simply because of a disability or challenging behavior. Instead, the teachers will partner with the family to help the child be successful. For example, the kitchen staff will rearrange the menu to make sure that children with significant allergies are not put at risk. The administrator will work to train staff to make sure they are prepared to support the children in their classrooms. Not every child-care program operates this way, and it's important for staff members to know that your program has an inclusive priority.

Requirements for Health and Safety

Although health and safety policies refer to all families, this section of your handbooks may need to be adapted to discuss the needs of students with disabilities and diagnosed medical conditions. For example, it is important to include information on emergency medical plans for children with chronic health conditions such as asthma and epilepsy. Parents (and a treating physician) need to offer information on how a child is to be treated during an emergency and what the staff need to do when responding to an emergency. All staff members working with that child need to be updated on those procedures.

When addressing emergency drills, have a plan to assist children with disabilities. Are there physical adaptations that need to be made to help the children leave the building quickly and safely? Will an emergency drill cause a child with a disability to panic? If so, how does the staff need to help that child practice the drill to be prepared in the event of a real emergency? How will the center support children with food allergies and life-threatening allergies? How can the program support a child with a disability as he or she begins to toilet train? (See page 71 for an example of how one child-care program handled this in their handbook.) You can address all of these issues in both the family and staff handbooks with the option for families to set up a conference to discuss the issue in more depth.

> **ABC Child Development Center Family Handbook: Toilet Training**
>
> Toilet training is an individualized skill, and no child enrolled at ABC Child Development Center will be penalized for not being toilet trained by a certain age. The teachers will work with the family to toilet train the child when he or she is ready. To begin toilet training, the child must be able to sit independently on the toilet and be able to identify when he or she may need to use the restroom.
>
> If a child is not toilet trained, that will not prohibit the child from moving to a preschool classroom. If a child is preschool-aged, he or she will not have a soiled diaper changed on a changing table. Instead, the child will lie down on a nonporous mat that can be cleaned with a bleach solution. This will prevent the teacher from being injured from picking up the child, and it will allow the child to have more privacy without being changed on a table where his or her peers can view.

Curriculum

Be sure your family and staff handbooks address how your program individualizes the curriculum for all the children, to help each child be as successful as possible. It is also critical to address developmental assessments and how that information will help the teachers implement the best possible curriculum for the children enrolled. Because many children struggle with transitions throughout the school day, it can be helpful to families to address how the daily classroom transitions will be handled and how a child will transition to a new classroom environment.

Behavior-Management Policies

In the section on the center's behavior-management policies, focus most of the discussion on positive behavior management and redirection. Consider including your center's policies on biting, aggressive behavior, and suspension and expulsion.

Addressing suspension and expulsion does not mean that your center practices suspension and expulsion. For example, a Head Start partnership child-care program would have a policy that says children will not be suspended or expelled. Instead, child-care professionals will work with the children and the families to eliminate negative behaviors and help the child be successful in the classroom setting.

If your program does have a suspension and expulsion policy, include a step-by-step description in the family handbook so that families understand what the process looks like. If the policy states that a child will not be expelled as long as the family is working with the child-care program and seeking behavioral supports as needed, then the handbook should specifically state that the family must seek therapeutic support for the child to maintain enrollment if challenging behaviors continue to be a problem. Concrete information is going to help the family members understand their accountability while protecting the child-care program at the same time.

ABC Child Development Center Family Handbook: Discipline and Guidance

Positive Redirection

ABC Child Development Center believes in positive redirection and natural consequences instead of punishment. We do not use time-out or take away playground time because a child didn't clean up a mess. Instead, we try to encourage a child when we see her making positive choices. If a child throws a block, then the natural consequence is to lose the opportunity to play in the block area for a while until the child can show that she understands the center rules.

We also attempt to avoid putting unnecessary rules and expectations on the children, so it is easier for the children not to get in trouble. For example, there is not one specific way that a child must sit at circle time. If a child is having a hard time with a classroom rule, then we try to give him two reasonable choices that give him some control in the situation.

We do **not** use:

- Physical punishment or rough handling
- Behavior charts
- A time-out chair
- Shaming, name-calling, or ridiculing
- Food or physical activity as a reward or punishment

We **do** use:

- A quiet corner that a child can choose to use when he is overstimulated
- Movement breaks outside of the classroom
- Sensory work to help regulate the child's body
- Redirection to another area of the classroom or to another group of peers
- Discussions on why a behavior might hurt or upset a friend

If a child has a pattern of negative behaviors, our program will partner with the family to find the root of the problem and establish a system of interventions that can be used at home and at school. We also partner with pediatric therapists and behavior specialists in our community. We invite specialists into the classroom to evaluate whether the classroom set up and teaching strategies are benefitting all the children in the classroom.

Aggressive Behavior

ABC Child Development Center recognizes that it is developmentally normal when a toddler bites a teacher or a peer. If biting becomes a reoccurring problem, then the family and the classroom teachers may need to meet for a conference to create a plan for how to reduce the problem behavior. If biting continues after accommodations are made in the classroom, then the teachers may recommend a developmental evaluation, particularly if the biting seems to be a symptom of a greater need the child is experiencing. If the family is working with the center to reduce the problem behavior, then the center will continue the child's enrollment.

We understand that young children may occasionally hit or kick to communicate with teachers or peers; however, if the behavior becomes a pattern, the family will need to work with the teachers to eliminate the problem behaviors as soon as possible. Our program will facilitate parent-teacher conferences and/or behavior referrals to give the child all the support that he or she needs. As long as the family continues to work with the teachers to eliminate the behaviors, the child will still be enrolled in the classroom setting.

When a young child is demonstrating an aggressive behavior such as biting or hitting, then we may require that one of the classroom teachers closely shadow the child for several days to intervene and break the habit. This means that the teacher will need to be close enough to the child to step in quickly before the child can bite, and then redirect the behavior. The teacher may also need to create strategies to use when redirecting the child, such as using the same phrases each time or reading picture books that demonstrate the positive behavior that the teacher is trying to demonstrate to the child.

Classroom Arrangements that Deter Negative Behavior

Some classroom designs may increase negative behaviors. For example, if there are not enough materials for every child to share in a center, or if the furniture arrangement offers a wide-open space where children are tempted to run or engage indoor active behavior. Teachers need to be willing to rearrange the classroom as one way to address behavior problems. Teachers can also use instruments such as the *Infant/Toddler Environment Rating Scale* (Harms, Cryer, Clifford, and Yazejian, 2017) or the *Early Childhood Environment Rating Scale* (Harms, Clifford, and Cryer, 2014) to make sure that the classroom is set up to facilitate learning.

Job Descriptions

Staff members must understand from the time of hire (or from the start of the transition) that caring for children with disabilities will be part of their job expectations. That means that each staff member's job description may change. Depending on the changes you and your management team decide to make, staff members may need to

- learn about differentiating curriculum based on the needs of the children,
- take trainings on how to support children and families with special needs,
- learn how to set up a classroom environment that can serve children of different ability levels, and
- understand that their jobs include collaborating with the families of children who need classroom accommodations.

All of these new policies should be outlined in the staff handbook.

All child-care programs should have job descriptions written out for the director, teachers, assistant teachers, floaters, and kitchen staff. The difference at an inclusive child-care program is that each job description should include information about working with children with different abilities. Staff should be willing to find alternative ways to teach children with different learning styles. Teachers should individualize lesson plans to help children who are working on learning different skills. Teachers in preschool classrooms may have to assist students with hygiene and personal-care routines if a child is not yet completely toilet trained or is still struggling with feeding skills. Classroom staff also need to be willing to work on developmental assessments and observations of young children to influence lesson plan design.

Program Operations

The program operations section of a staff handbook typically includes the day-to-day work that a staff member will be responsible for. In an inclusive program, this is often the first section of the staff handbook that begins to address making accommodations for children with disabilities. That may mean lowering adult-to-child ratios, changing the physical access point of the playground, or changes to mealtimes to make sure that every child's needs are met. The theme of inclusion should be woven throughout the daily operations.

Discipline and Guidance

It is essential that child-care staff understand the program behavior-guidance process. Many adults will discipline children in the same manner that they were disciplined as children, and typically, classroom discipline techniques differ from those at home. All staff members must understand what a positive redirection system is and that positive redirection is a priority over negative consequences. If teachers have no experience with this type of system, then their orientation training should include examples of how to implement this system in the classroom, as well as watching a mentor teacher demonstrate this in the classroom setting.

Staff members must have some basic understanding of child development milestones so that young children are not disciplined for skills that they are not yet developmentally capable of mastering. If a center does not use time-out, it is important to share that information with the teacher before they begin working in the classroom. Teachers should also receive some information on why behaviors like biting or hitting are developmentally appropriate and how to deter those behaviors in the classroom.

When child-care programs take the time to evaluate each policy to determine its impact on families of children with disabilities, then they can solidify the policies to implement in their child-care programs. Using the staff and family handbooks to display those policies gives a solid method of communication for individuals to refer to throughout their association with the child-care programs. This also provides accountability for the child-care program when they may feel tempted to not enforce a policy for one family but enforce it for another.

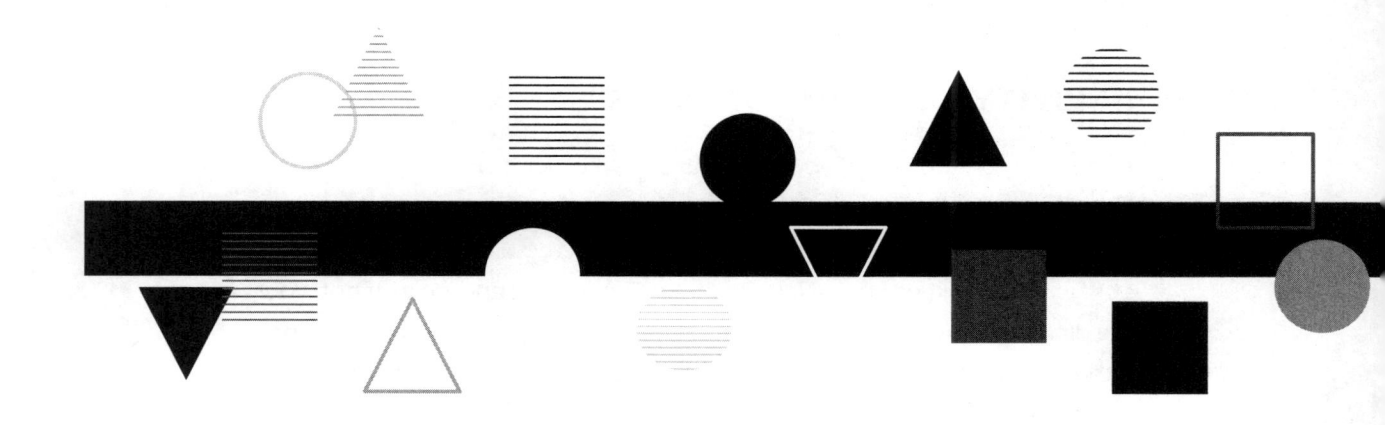

CHAPTER 6

Creating Accommodations

In addition to setting new policies for your inclusive child-care program, you may also need to make specific changes to the classroom, the materials, or teaching approaches so that each child has an opportunity to participate in all classroom activities. An accommodation will take away the barriers for a child with special needs so that they can have full access to learning and participating in the classroom. Some accommodations may be specific to a particular child, but other accommodations can be beneficial to every child in the classroom.

This chapter looks at a number of accommodations to consider:

- Facility accommodations
- Classroom materials
- Curriculum accommodations
- Behavior-management accommodations
- Accommodations for meals

FACILITY ACCOMMODATIONS

Depending on the age of your building and whether it was originally built to be an early childhood education program, your facility may require some accommodations to serve as an inclusive child care. Can children and staff with disabilities access or use the building independently? If not, your building may need a wheelchair ramp to enter the building or an elevator if the building has more than one floor so that children with mobility disabilities can move from floor to floor.

Access can also be an issue on the playground. If the playground surface is comprised of mulch chips, shredded rubber, or another uneven surface, it can be difficult for children with disabilities to move around the playground without falling. Playgrounds with cushioned surfaces that surround the large climbing structures of swings reduce injury, but not all of those surfaces make it easy for children with physical disabilities to move across. The most accessible playground surface is poured rubber, which can be expensive. Some child-care programs may have to raise money or dedicate a large investment to make sure that children have access to all parts of the facility, indoors and outdoors. Programs should also consider whether children can access the equipment on the playground. Not every piece of playground equipment has to be accessible, but enough equipment must be accessible so that children with disabilities can enjoy playing outdoors.

Once you've determined that the children can access the classroom, review the accessibility of furniture and furniture design. The height of the classroom tables can be an issue. Depending on the abilities of the children, you may need to adjust your tables. If a child is in a wheelchair, then the tabletops need to align with the height of the wheelchair so that the child can roll up to the table and engage in activities there. Some children may not be able to get up and down into chairs easily. Just as an adult may have a standing desk at work, a child may need a higher table to work on a flat surface without sitting in a chair. Many activities, such as puzzles or blocks, in the early childhood classroom are designed for the floor. If a child cannot access the floor easily, then consider adding a small table to the block or puzzle area, so the child can still participate in all the classroom activities.

You may also need to adapt the design and placement of the furniture. Typically, teachers use furniture to section off the classroom and create designated areas so that children do not get overly excited and run around the classroom. If an inclusive classroom has children with limited mobility, then the floor plan may need to be more open. A child in a wheelchair or a child using a walker or crutches may not be able to navigate the turns and corners if a classroom is divided by shelving and tables into distinct centers. Instead, create clear pathways throughout the room that all children can navigate.

Look at the seating in the classroom to ensure that it is accessible to all children who use the space. Not every child can sit in a typical chair with their back and knees at ninety-degree angles. In an inclusive classroom, you'll need to consider a variety of alternative seating. Some children may need to sit in a more relaxed position closer to the floor; in this case, provide them with beanbag chairs or wedge seats. For children who need a seat with more movement, try stools that rock, such as Hokki stools, or sensory pads that will allow children to move back and forth to receive more sensory stimulation. Other children may need to use a traditional chair with props or bolsters so that their muscles can begin to support their weight in new positions. If a child has low muscle tone, adapt the chair by placing a rougher surface on the seat, such as the material used on a no-skid mat for the inside of a bathtub, so that the child will not slide off the surface.

Along with the furniture, you may also need to make adjustments to your classroom's temperature and lighting. Some light bulbs, especially those with higher contrasts where a child can actually see the oscillation, can be overstimulating to children with disabilities, especially children with neurological disorders. Flashing or strobing lights can trigger seizures in children with epilepsy (Bullock, 2017). At the same time, children with visual impairments may need increased lighting in the room so that they can see distinct differences in contrast (Bullock, 2017). Fluctuations in temperature can also be challenging for young children with special needs, especially infants and toddlers. Many infants who are prone to seizures can have febrile seizures when their body temperature increases too quickly (National Institute of Neurological Disorders and Stroke, 2023). In older buildings, keeping the temperature at a consistent level can be challenging, so it is important for teachers and administrators to know the medical background of all the children.

CLASSROOM MATERIALS

Even when classroom materials and toys are marketed to young children, they may be designed only for children who are typically developing. All children should have access to age-appropriate classroom materials that they can use. For example, if a preschool student has difficulty with fine-motor skills, he should not be using infant and toddler toys. Activities for the child should be age-appropriate, and the teachers should create accommodations to help him use them.

You can easily adapt many classroom materials to help with stability. For example, if children have a hard time keeping their art paper still, use masking tape to stick the paper to the table or provide the children with easels to hold the paper in place and to let them draw or paint at an angle, which is usually easier for holding a marker or paintbrush. You can use this type of adaptation for blocks or other stacking materials by placing Velcro tape on the sides of blocks so that children can stabilize the block to the surface and more easily stack materials on top.

Fine-motor skills can also affect a child's ability to manipulate a glue bottle. If children can't create a collage because they can't control the glue, use clear contact paper as the base of the collage so children can stick materials to the contact paper instead of squeezing and spreading the glue. If a child has difficulty using markers or crayons, adapt the thickness of the marker by wrapping it in foam and making the surface area thicker, helping them grip the marker with more stability. A teacher could also adapt the pages of a book by applying a paperclip so that the pages are easier to turn for small fingers.

You can also adapt large-muscle activities according to the child's needs. For example, if a child is not tall enough to use a school tricycle, attach rectangular blocks to the pedals so that the child has a stable target to push. Adaptive seating also falls into this category. Children who have weaker stomach or leg muscles may want to be positioned to lie down on the floor while looking at a book so that they can still hold it up. Children with weaker finger strength may prefer board books or supersized books with thicker pages, so they can turn the pages independently.

Children with visual impairments may be better able to complete a puzzle or table activity if it is placed on top of a light table. The contrast between the lights and the materials enables children to see the materials more clearly and find ways to manipulate the pieces. Smartboards and computers may help them master activities that children with typical sight can do with hands-on manipulatives. Audiobooks can be enjoyed by children with and without visual impairments. Although most high-quality early childhood classrooms discourage the overuse of technology, it can be a great asset for children with limited sight. Children with speech delays may use tablets with graphic pictures to communicate to teachers or peers, or the same pictures on a tablet may help children with autism understand the classroom routines.

You can also adapt other classroom materials to decrease the noise level for children who have issues with too much sensory stimulation. This can be as simple as putting tennis balls over the bottoms of the chair legs so they slide quietly, turning off the volume of automated toys, or making sure that materials are in good repair so that they do not squeak unnecessarily. Some children may already be overwhelmed in a classroom with multiple children all moving around at one time, so any small adaptation to a material to limit unnecessary noise can be very helpful. Also consider creating a quiet area for the children. This can be a large cardboard box or tent that children can hide in to isolate themselves from the rest of the classroom. The ultimate purpose is to make accommodations so that the classroom is as quiet as possible.

CURRICULUM ACCOMMODATIONS

Curriculum accommodations remove barriers to the lesson plans and the content that teachers are sharing with the students. This isn't an accommodation to the classroom materials, but rather an accommodation to how the teacher shares information with the children to remove the barrier that prevents the child from understanding the lesson and participating fully in the curriculum.

Some of the most obvious accommodations for young children are provided by medical professionals. For example, children with hearing impairments can use hearing aids. Assistive technology, such as a table with picture communication, can help children who may otherwise be nonverbal to communicate. Teachers can also teach sign language to help children communicate when they cannot communicate orally.

Another important accommodation is to break down the lesson plans into simpler steps. If classroom activities have multiple steps, the child may not be able to think about all the steps at one time and decide what to do next. If a child is doing a puzzle, for example, you may want to offer one piece at a time, which enables the child to focus on one decision without getting distracted.

BEHAVIOR-MANAGEMENT ACCOMMODATIONS

In addition to providing curriculum and materials accommodations, an early childhood classroom moving to an inclusive program will also need to adapt how it manages young children's behaviors. Consider incorporating the following:

- Movement breaks
- One-on-one support
- Peer support
- Positive feedback
- Consistent routines
- Appropriate expectations

Movement Breaks

People often assume that young children can sit still for a long period of time and take in information by listening to the teacher talk. Ask any preschool teacher, and they'll tell you that this is not a correct assumption. Even in a classroom that is developmentally appropriate and play based, some children will need additional accommodations to manage their own behavior and regulate their bodies.

One simple accommodation is for children with sensory or behavioral disabilities to have additional movement breaks throughout the school day, which can help them refocus after expending energy. Movement breaks can include heavy lifting. When a child does heavy lifting or hard work, the deep pressure can stimulate the proprioceptive system of the body and give children more body awareness (Springbrook Autism Behavioral Health, 2017). Activities that can assist with heavy lifting or hard work include asking children to:

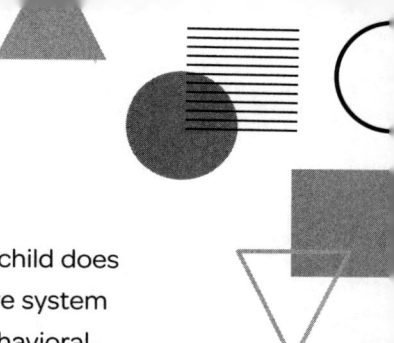

- Pull a wagon with classroom materials or a peer taking a ride
- Move furniture around the classroom
- Carry the classroom backpack to the playground
- Play tug-of-war
- Lie on their tummies (for infants)
- Climb
- Lift heavy classroom materials

One-on-One Support

Having a child sit next to the teacher or paraeducator in the classroom can assist with behavior management, because it can help the child to feel safe and to focus more closely on the classroom activities. Regarding the classroom centers, children may show more interest if you incorporate a child's favorite toy into different classroom activities to attract the child's interest. If you are working with a child who struggles to participate in daily classroom activities, incorporating their favorite toy into the lesson plan may redirect their interest.

Peer Support

Encouraging children who are typically developing to provide support to their peers who have special needs is a win for all involved: the children who are typically developing, the children with special needs, and the teachers. For example, working with typically developing children to be helpers to students who need more support can be particularly useful during classroom transitions like cleaning up or moving to the playground. If a child with a mobility delay has a peer helper guide them to the playground, then not only can relationships develop between the children but the teacher is more available to help students who may have greater needs.

Guiding social groups to play together in classroom centers is a way for peers to model social behaviors. If there are certain children having arguments while they play, guided group play may allow children to create new relationships and enjoy group interactions with a different group of peers. For example, the teacher can sit in the dramatic play area and narrate as the children play. "I can tell that Angie is frustrated. If you are frustrated, maybe you should tell Tomás why you are frustrated. Did something upset you?" This may not be an activity that you use all the time, but it can be helpful when emotions are heightened. Children can be placed in "teams" for short activities to assist with sharing, taking turns, and cooperative play.

Positive Feedback

When teachers see children demonstrating appropriate behavior in the classroom, they should offer immediate and positive feedback. Children are more likely to identify the behavior for which they are being praised if the praise happens immediately following the positive behavior. The more time that passes before the teacher offers praise, the more likely that the child will not know what the praise is for. When children are encouraged for positive behavior, they are more likely to duplicate the behavior. A positive behavior-management system is always much more productive than using punishment for a negative behavior since that only teaches the child what not to do.

Consistent Routines

Another way to break down behavior barriers is to follow the same sequences each day. A daily schedule is important to the classroom, but the routine is more important than the times used in the schedule. When children know the daily order of events, then they know what to anticipate each day. Knowing what comes next in the day can decrease anxiety and help the children ease through transitions. If the most challenging transitions of the day, such as moving from playground time to lunch time to nap time, have a consistent routine, then the children are more likely to be successful.

Picture schedules and charts displayed in the classroom can help children understand what will happen next. A picture schedule for the entire day may be overwhelming for some students, so consider limiting the chart to show just two to three pictures at a time. You can then update items throughout the day to show the child the current activity and the next one or two activities that will follow.

Appropriate Expectations

Teachers also need to make sure that they set appropriate expectations for their students. One of the easiest expectations to alter is how much time the teacher gives a child to complete a desired task. Even in a one-on-one lesson with a teacher, a child with a disability may need additional time to complete a task. The teacher also may need to give additional prompts to help the child complete the task.

Some children become comfortable playing the same activities each day, but this practice doesn't help a child to learn new skills. To encourage a child to try something new, make small alterations to the child's play. For example, if a child wants to build with blocks each day, slowly add materials to the block area and encourage the child to add them to her current play. This could mean adding matchbox cars to see if the child might build a car garage or a racetrack. You may need to demonstrate some of the new activities first, but modeling new activities may encourage the child to try something new.

ACCOMMODATIONS FOR MEALS

Your program should review meal accommodations for children with disabilities and special health-care needs on a case-by-case basis. The food substitution should be based on a prescription written by a licensed physician. The school kitchen staff may not disregard a prescription or medical order from a child's physician. If an alternative food is needed, it must fulfill the same nutritional requirement as the food that the child is unable to eat. For example, if a child is not able to drink cow's milk due to an allergy, then an appropriate substitute may be almond milk or oat milk. If your program is not able to offer all the required substitutions, collaborate with the family to make sure that the child receives the proper nutrition throughout the school day.

Some children with a disability require feeding therapy, so there may be some who cannot eat certain textures. In those cases, again, the child needs to be fed a substitute food that meets the same nutritional requirements as the food the child is unable to eat. In this case, the physician or a licensed feeding therapist can write an official statement describing the textures that are challenging for the child. If the consistency of the food is an issue, then it may be possible for the item to be blended or pureed so the child can eat it.

If a child has a life-threatening allergy, it is not only essential to prevent the child from eating that item but also to make sure that there is no cross-contamination between the child's food and the allergen. In some cases, the allergy may be so life-threatening that the center chooses to remove the item from the entire school menu to make sure that the child does not suffer from anaphylaxis.

■ ■ ■

There is no specific set of accommodations that must be used in an inclusive classroom setting. All the changes that teachers use to support their students are based on the individual group of students that they have in that classroom. Teachers can adjust their teaching style and their classroom design to support children as needed, and the child's special-education support team can offer guidance to help with creative solutions.

A Pediatric Occupational Therapist in the Classroom

Casey has been a pediatric occupational therapist for fifteen years. She often visits child-care programs to do therapy sessions with her clients so that the therapy takes place in the child's natural environment. Children who attend child care spend the majority of their days in the child-care program. Because Casey offers on-site therapy, she has visited hundreds of child-care programs in her hometown and the surrounding counties.

I have been a pediatric occupational therapist for fifteen years. I work in a pediatric therapy practice with two speech pathologists, a physical therapist, two other occupational therapists, and a mental-health professional. We all focus on working with children from birth through age twelve. Many of our patients see more than one therapist in our practice due to having a complex condition that needs multiple types of therapy. Our practice has an individual treatment office for each of the therapists, but we also share a large therapy gym where children can work on large-muscle activities and social interactions with other patients. I spend 90 percent of my treatment time working in our treatment office. The only time I leave is when I work with our Early Steps clients.

The most common question I'm asked is, "What does an occupational therapist do?" The general answer is that an occupational therapist is a therapist who helps you do your occupation. For young children, that means I help them learn how to go to school, function as a member of their families, and learn to regulate their bodies and their emotions. When children come to my practice to see me, I am often helping them express their emotions, demonstrate hygiene skills, interact with adults and their peers, control their muscles and their bodies, and learn pre-academic skills that will help them be successful in school.

My state offers Early Steps, an early intervention program for children who are younger than three years of age and show a significant developmental delay in one or more areas. This program is set up to be a home-visiting program to meet the families in their natural setting, and for some children who are enrolled full-time in a child-care program, their natural setting is their child-care program. Pediatric therapists from practices all over our state participate in the Early Steps program. Our participation helps increase enrollment numbers for our practice because when those patients graduate out of Early Steps at age three, many of the families like to stay with our therapists.

If one of my Early Steps patients is enrolled full-time in a child-care program, then that is where I visit that child for therapy sessions. There are a few exceptions to that rule. Some child-care programs do not want visitors to enter their program, so in that case, the family and I have to work out an alternative. That can be really hard on the family, because it usually means that one of the adults in the home has to take time off work, which can eat up a large amount of paid time off if I visit the child every week.

Some families will deliberately rearrange their work schedules so that I can visit their child at their home with the parent present. This is usually because the parent is interested in seeing the strategies that I use in therapy so that they can use them at home. Although I applaud this type of dedication, most families do not have the flexibility to arrange their schedules this way. When I do see a child in the child-care program, I typically send home notes for the family and handouts about any exercises or treatments that I used, so that the family members can use them at home too. Another benefit of doing a therapy session at the child-care program is that I can also train the child-care providers on how to use the strategies, so they can help the child in the classroom when I am not there. That can be a huge help to the classroom, since most of the child-care providers have limited special-education experience.

At this point in my career, I have worked in almost every child-care program in our community that will allow Early Steps therapists to come into their programs. Outside of my professional life, I am also the mother of two children. I can tell you both as a professional and as a mother, there are huge differences among child-care programs in my town. There are high-quality programs in which I would have loved to enroll my own children, and there are programs that make me cringe as soon as I walk in the door. One of the biggest differences I see when I enter these programs is how the teachers interact with children who have disabilities. Many child-care providers do not have special-education training. That is one of the main reasons that I work with the Early Steps program, so that I can help these teachers understand how to support children with differences. However, many of the lower-quality child-care programs don't know how to bring out the best in the typically developing children, much less in the students with disabilities. Some of their classroom practices are appropriate for older elementary school students, but two- and three-year-old children are struggling to be in a classroom with unrealistic expectations. If the classroom were set up to be developmentally appropriate for the age of the children enrolled, then it would also be more accommodating to children who have a developmental delay.

One of the practices that causes both children who have special needs and those who do not to struggle the most is behavior charts. I see these all the time, and they come in many different packages. Some are decorated like rainbows, and children move down the colors of the rainbow as they have additional negative behaviors. Other charts look like stoplights, and the children move from green to red. Some teachers allow children to move back up the chart if they improve their behaviors throughout the day, but unfortunately most teachers only allow a child to move further down the behavior chart with no chance of starting over. Most behavior charts are a clean slate each day when the student arrives, but I have seen behavior charts that focus on the whole week, so if a student behaves poorly on Monday, then the rest of the week is automatically a loss.

No matter how the chart looks or the length of time that it is used, a behavior chart is punitive. The child is scolded for negative behaviors with no acknowledgement for the dozens of positive behaviors that have occurred during the course of the day. The chart is also public. Everyone in the classroom can judge the child's behavior and compare that one student to every other child in the room. For students with anxiety or with social-emotional delays, a public discipline system can be the greatest punishment of all, even if a child is not the student who is in "trouble."

Circle time is another common practice in many child-care programs that can be problematic for young children, particularly for those with special needs. If circle time is too long or is used for drills, memorization, and rote teaching, then it is not appropriate for young children. When implemented inappropriately, learning is not happening; a battle to get everyone to sit quietly in the same position and keep their hands to themselves is underway.

There are better ways to help children focus. For example, I often have children go down the slide headfirst or swing on their bellies. I do this not to cause chaos but to help children feel their bodies in space and learn to take control of their muscles. When children engage in these types of behaviors and feel their bodies fall through space, they are able to learn to control their muscles and balance. Small bodies are not programmed for stillness. Children who need to rock back and forth, lie on their stomachs, or move their heads from side to side to listen are following the lead of their bodies. This behavior is not something that should be punished.

Research-based early childhood education programs are training teachers that most of the learning should happen during play, when children can interact with classroom materials and ask open-ended questions. Unfortunately, not all teachers have been trained this way. When children are allowed to learn through play, and play takes up the largest portion of the school day, then the differences between children with and without disabilities is less noticeable. Children will naturally learn at their own speed, and teachers can support them in small groups or one-on-one lessons. When I am in a program that supports children with disabilities, this is the type of learning that I see, and there are far fewer behavior problems because children are not forced to be still and remain quiet.

Another area that concerns me when I am visiting child-care programs is how different programs discipline their students. For a child with a disability, it is best to redirect the child and simply tell them why the behavior is not acceptable. For a two-year-old, I may simply say, "No hit." That may be all the child can comprehend. For an older preschool student, I may try to show the child how they have upset a peer and then direct them to another activity for the time being. It can be challenging for an inexperienced teacher to remain patient and redirect a child who is repeatedly demonstrating a negative behavior. It may appear that the child is not listening, but a young child may need many redirections to learn a new behavior. I find that, often, the teacher does not see quick results from redirection and feels that a strategy needs to be more severe to work.

When discipline practices escalate in a child-care program, all the children in the classroom tend to suffer, especially the children with disabilities. Many child-care programs will use time-out as a disciple practice. This usually means that a child is removed from the rest of the classroom to sit alone for a short amount of time. This practice was initially created to help children calm down when they were frustrated or upset, but now teachers use it as a discipline tool. Although many high-quality child-care programs have moved away from using time-out, if it is used correctly, it is only used for a short amount of time. The standard is to use one-minute of time-out per year of the child's age. So, a three-year-old child would not need a time-out longer than three minutes.

When my patient is enrolled in an inclusive child-care program, the center or the family child-care home is supportive of me being there from the moment that I contact the administrator. Their goal is to support the children enrolled in their program, and if that means a therapist visiting the classroom, then they will make the arrangements for that to happen. They also attempt to follow all protocol to make sure that their students are safe, so they have all the necessary background checks in place and follow the program's confidentiality policies. Many programs ask for an introductory meeting with me and the parents to make sure that they fully understand the child's needs and the overall goals of the therapy. The teachers are involved in all of the communication as well, to make sure that they can implement the therapeutic strategies once I leave the classroom.

Most inclusive classrooms have a play-based learning environment. They may still have a classroom circle time, but it generally lasts only five to ten minutes for the youngest students and up to fifteen minutes for preschoolers. Circle time usually focuses on saying hello to all the children and introducing them to the new classroom activities for the day. Inclusive classrooms typically give some children with disabilities the opportunity to decline coming to circle time. When I see this in the classroom, most of the children are sitting in the classroom circle, but one or two students with more significant needs are allowed to move around the classroom quietly if sitting and focusing for a short amount of time is more challenging for them. I have also seen alternative seating at circle time in inclusive classrooms. Some children sit with their legs crossed, but others may use therapeutic wiggle seats or beanbag chairs or even lie on their stomachs. As long as they keep their bodies to themselves, then how they sit at the circle is not criticized.

After circle time, the teachers supervise the classroom during free play. They also move around the room to do small-group activities or one-on-one lessons with the students. This allows the teachers to help children with more advanced language interactions as well as children who benefit from an adapted curriculum, such as those with disabilities and those who are more advanced. My favorite lessons to watch are when the teachers can ask children how and why questions, such as "Why did the block tower fall down?" or "How is the paint changing color when you mix it up?" These types of lessons allow the children to learn more than just flashcard memorization skills. They start to problem solve and can experiment to see if their theories actually work. This can be done with very young students, depending on how complicated the questions are. One of my favorite activities in the toddler classroom is to play with the jack-in-the-box and ask my patient, "Where did Jack go?" I love watching the toddler try to figure out where Jack is before we crank the handle.

Of course, I am always grateful for child-care programs that make physical adjustments to the classroom for my patients who have more noticeable disabilities. A wheelchair ramp on the playground for a student in a walker or a lower table in the two-year-old room for a child who is in a small wheelchair is a huge help. Those types of modifications are often very expensive, but they are investments that can last a long time and serve many different children. The reality is that most students enrolled in child-care programs do not have physical disabilities. The majority have invisible disabilities, and the accommodations may be more challenging because the teachers must change all of their teaching practices to support them. A one-time change to furniture is simpler than changing teaching practices every day; however, inclusive teaching practices end up benefitting all the children in the classroom. As an observer and a parent, if my children had disabilities, those are the programs that I would want them to be a part of. I just want the teachers to meet children where they are developmentally and teach them from that point. Ultimately, that is what the inclusive classroom does.

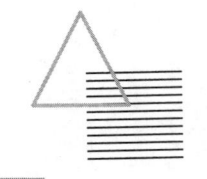

CHAPTER 7

Supporting Teaching Staff in the Inclusive Classroom

The most valuable asset that any child-care program has is its teaching staff. Although beautiful buildings and aesthetically pleasing classrooms can be enticing to families, no one will leave a child with a teacher they don't trust. In inclusive classrooms, teachers will face challenging situations and need to be dedicated to the mission of the child-care program. It is essential to find the best staff members to work with the children in your program.

Once you've hired a talented team of educators to work with children with and without disabilities, you'll need to support those teachers. One key aspect of keeping staff members at a program is creating positive relationships among the teachers and helping them feel valued. That foundation allows the employees to feel like a united team. Once the staff are working together for the same cause, it is essential for your management team to ensure that everyone has the tools they need to be successful in their positions, which may include the following:

- Training and professional development
- Specialized support and teaching assistants
- Access to and time for developmental assessments
- Support in using new teaching styles
- Adequate planning time
- Opportunities for self-care

TRAINING AND PROFESSIONAL DEVELOPMENT

The support that teachers in the inclusive classroom need most is strategies to work with children who have disabilities. This means that every teacher—whether a lead or an assistant teacher, full-time or part-time—needs training on how to work with children who have specialized needs. Many training programs for the Child Development Associate's certificate or college teacher-certification programs only briefly talk about special education, so teachers in an inclusive program will need additional training after they are hired.

An inclusive child-care program can offer one thing that a textbook cannot: hands-on experience. Simply reading about different disabilities will not give teachers real-life experience; they need to interact with children in the classroom setting. To know how to handle accommodations and challenging behaviors, however, a newer teacher needs a mentor who can guide them through tricky situations. A teacher with general-education training can start off in the inclusive classroom as an assistant teacher and learn from the experienced teacher. Of course, this means that your program must have skilled teachers who can pass their years of experience on to newer staff members. Some veteran teachers may not feel comfortable with teaching high-need students and mentoring a co-teacher at the same time. Your child-care program will need to determine which members of the teaching staff are the most skilled at assisting younger teachers and perhaps offer them a promotion or a financial bonus for being willing to mentor new staff members.

An alternative is to have a teacher or administrator who is not in the classroom coach the newer teacher. In this situation, the mentor could meet with the newer teacher after classroom hours. The new teacher could come to the mentoring session prepared to ask questions about situations that came up during the week. The mentor teacher could also focus the sessions on specific coaching topics and ask the new teacher to use certain teaching strategies in the classroom during the week. After the new teacher implements the skill, they return to the following coaching session with reflections on how the technique worked and if further accommodations need to be made.

In addition to mentoring new staff, you'll also need to assess the backgrounds and skill development of all the teachers in the child-care program, including the veteran teaching staff. Many administrators will use a self-assessment that each teacher fills out to determine the areas of content with which they feel the least comfortable. The self-evaluation may include lesson planning, behavior-management strategies, general knowledge of disabilities, working with families, or developing and following IEPs. After your teachers identify areas of weakness, review the information individually and as a whole.

You may notice significant trends in the staff self-assessments that show most teachers need training in certain areas. Consider planning a training for the whole staff during a staff in-service day. Focusing on a training for the whole staff can be beneficial for the teachers, because they realize that they are learning a skill together and they all have room for improvement. In an inclusive child-care program, group trainings should focus on supporting children with disabilities, because that is what makes the program unique. In particular, consider offering regular training to staff on how to deal with challenging behaviors. Children will typically exhibit behaviors that they know they can get away with in the classroom, so it is important for teachers to understand how to design and manage a classroom in a way that discourages aggression and other unwanted behaviors.

Trainings that focus on inclusive classrooms can also be hard to find, so it is better for the director to make sure that everyone is receiving those trainings. These trainings may include in-depth instruction on specific disabilities, trainings on how to manage challenging behaviors, or instruction on how to support parents of children with disabilities.

After reviewing each staff member's self-evaluation, look at individual skills with which each teacher feels less comfortable. Combining the teacher's self-evaluation with your observations of the classroom can help you pinpoint areas in which the teacher really does need support. Use the classroom observation along with the self-evaluation, because some educators are always going to be exceptionally hard on themselves. They may feel poorly prepared, even when they have a highly developed skill set. After you have identified growth areas for all the teaching staff, meet with each staff member to create a professional-development plan. This plan should not be excessive; focus on three to four goals at the most. Ask the teacher to pick an area to focus on and then to choose some specific short- or long-term goals within that area. Short-term goals may be completed in six weeks to three months, but long-term goals may take the entire year.

If the teacher is focusing on lesson planning, then short-term goals may include practice in adapting individual lesson plans for children above and below the typical developmental milestone. Another short-term goal may include creating lesson plans that appeal to one child in the classroom who does not seem to engage with any of the classroom materials. A long-term goal may include studying the lesson plans of other teachers in the child-care program to see how they create their lessons for children with different abilities.

Once a teacher has established some annual goals, focus their individual training hours on those topics. Assist the teacher with looking for trainings that align with the program's vision and mission statement. It is also important to support the training objectives. If you encourage an educator to attend a training on curriculum or behavior management, and the teacher comes back ready to implement those skills, you'll need to support that practice. If a teacher tries to implement changes in their classroom without the support of the program management, then the changes will not be successful.

This philosophy of follow-through shifts the director and the teachers away from a practice of attending trainings simply to meet the annual regulatory requirements. Of course, administrators must keep track of required training hours to meet the regulated minimum standards; however, that is not the point of professional development. The goal of professional training is to help the staff feel more prepared to complete their jobs and to help each employee become a lifelong learner. Valuing continued education is a priority that must be established with the administration and modeled for every staff member, so that the entire program can look forward to learning new skills.

SPECIALIZED SUPPORT AND TEACHING ASSISTANTS

Inclusive teaching is always a team effort. A classroom teacher is never expected to meet the needs of every child in the program. A child with disabilities has the opportunity to receive support from a general-education teacher, a special-education teacher, the program administrator, pediatric therapists, the child's family members, the child's doctors, and even community members who partner with the child-care program. Because one child can have so many different individuals supporting him or her, the child-care program does not simply consist of teachers and administrators.

In an inclusive child-care program, typically the lead teacher plays the roles of the general-education teacher and the special-education teacher. Most inclusive classroom teachers receive dual certification of some kind so that they are experts in child development and in special education. The lead teacher is usually not the only teacher in an inclusive classroom, because lower adult-to-child ratios usually require a co-teacher or an assistant teacher to be present to provide more individualized instruction.

An inclusive classroom may also utilize floating teachers or substitutes to be available to help when needed. Since many children with disabilities may be apprehensive about having new adults in the classroom, try to have a consistent substitute or additional floating teacher on staff who becomes acquainted with all of the children. It can also be helpful to have an adult ready to step into the classroom when a teacher may need to direct his or her attention to a tube feeding or a child's meltdown, or to take a child out of the classroom for a movement break. Children with disabilities may need more time out of the group classroom during the day than typically developing children do, so schedule enough staff members to make sure that movement breaks are possible.

Some child-care programs with inclusive classrooms may have a special-education coordinator or caseworker on staff. This individual can assist when children have IEP meetings with the public school system, can make sure that all developmental goals are recorded and documented, and can help teachers review developmental assessments that indicate a child may need a referral. The individual who fills this role needs special-education experience and a deep understanding of special-education laws and privacy acts. If teachers have additional support with IEP goals and progress, they can focus more on supporting children during classroom time. If a child-care program has a partnership with a local public school system, then the IEP caseworker will be supplied by the school district; however, the caseworker will not provide the additional support on goal tracking and documentation.

Inclusive child-care programs may hire pediatric therapists or may choose to partner with an organization, such as the public school system or a private pediatric therapy office, that will send pediatric therapists to work with the students with disabilities. Regardless of who pays these individuals, you will often see occupational therapists, physical therapists, speech pathologists, and behavior therapists working in the inclusive classroom setting. For children ages birth to five, the goal is to serve the children in the classroom as frequently as possible. The therapist may also spend time instructing the teachers on new techniques to use in the classroom to help the children meet new developmental goals. The therapists may be in the classroom to observe students who have been referred for a developmental evaluation or to re-evaluate a child who is already on their caseload.

Different child-care programs may add support roles to their center to make sure that all children are as successful as possible. Regardless of what new roles are added, all staff members still have the obligation to develop relationships with the children and families and keep all information confidential about the children, the families, and the child's health or disability. This level of professionalism should be required of all staff members, regardless of job responsibilities.

ACCESS TO AND TIME FOR DEVELOPMENTAL ASSESSMENTS

Inclusive child-care programs typically spend more time assessing the individual developmental needs of each child to be sure to teach the skills that will help the child advance developmentally. This happens for a few different reasons. First, the program's mission statement addresses providing the best possible education and care for children of all ability levels. That can only happen if a child's developmental delays are identified early and the child receives all the additional support possible. Child-care programs do not conduct formal evaluations, of course, but they can do informal screenings to show parents if a child is meeting the typical developmental milestones. If the screenings or assessment tools show that a child is lagging behind developmental milestones, then the teachers can share that pattern with the family, and the family can contact their pediatrician to ask how to proceed with help for the child.

Another reason that inclusive child-care programs frequently use developmental screenings and assessments is that children in the classroom can have a broad range of ability levels. Assessing each child gives the teacher better guidance on what skills each child needs to learn next. The assessment results can also help the teacher target small groups of children who are working on similar skills and can be gathered for lessons on similar content.

To evaluate all the information that is available to the teachers by using developmental assessments, teachers need to be properly trained on the developmental tools that the child-care program uses. Many child-care programs use screening tools as an introduction to a child's ability levels at the beginning of each new school year. A developmental screening takes a brief look at each of the developmental areas and focuses on four or five key skills in each area. In the early childhood classroom, these developmental areas usually include language, movement, thinking skills, independence skills, and social-emotional skills. The tool is a simple checklist or possibly a simple questionnaire for parents or families.

For a slightly more in-depth look at a child's development, the teacher may use a curriculum-based assessment, which is a developmental assessment that is specifically linked to skills the child would be doing in the daily classroom curriculum. For example, to assess the fine-motor skills of a preschool-aged child, you might observe whether the child can hold scissors correctly and cut a straight line or can use a crayon with a three-finger grasp. If the child is struggling with a specific skill, then the teacher would plan activities to allow the child to have an opportunity to practice.

The most advanced type of developmental assessment is a developmental evaluation conducted by a diagnostician or a pediatric therapist trained to do so. The results of the evaluation would specifically indicate whether the child had a delay in one or more areas of development and would be used to help create an IFSP or IEP for the public school system. Information from a developmental evaluation can also be used by the child's private health insurance company to decide whether the child qualifies for therapy through a private agency.

Even though the classroom teacher would not be conducting the evaluation, the results of the evaluation can significantly influence how the teacher supports the child in the classroom moving forward and what goals seem reasonable for the child over the next school year. Some children qualify for therapy through their health insurance company, but they don't qualify for special education through the public school system. In that case, it is key for the teacher to see the evaluation to create their own goals for the child.

SUPPORT IN USING NEW TEACHING STYLES

When teachers move from teaching in a traditional classroom environment to teaching in an inclusive classroom, they may find it challenging to learn new instruction styles. Many teachers struggle with changing the way that they teach in the same way that they would struggle with changing characteristics of their personality. Teaching style is very personal to a teacher, and it can feel overwhelming to learn a new way to relate to students in the classroom. To change teaching styles successfully, a teacher must make a concerted effort. Even if teacher is motivated to change, they will still need a great deal of support and encouraging feedback to be successful.

Depending on when and where teachers were initially trained, the lecture model may be one of their primary teaching approaches. This seems like a technique that would be reserved for secondary school; however, early childhood classrooms have their own version of the lecture technique: keeping young children seated for lengthy circle times. In this type of classroom, the teacher has been trained to impart their knowledge to the children in their classroom. Yet, it is actually more beneficial for teachers to support learning through classroom strategies that allow children to learn from the environment and from each other. Important teaching strategies in inclusive classrooms include the following:

- **Cooperative learning:** This is a student-centered approach to learning in which classroom engagement encourages the children to learn from one another. Children model for their peers, and they learn as they watch their peers explore the classroom (Johnson and Johnson, 2023).

- **Differentiated learning:** This is a strategy in which teachers adapt each lesson to the individual abilities of the children in the classroom. They also consider the different learning styles of the children, including visual, auditory, and kinesthetic learning (Wood, 2022).

- **Goal-setting:** In this type of strategy, the teacher consults with the child about what he or she would like to learn. The teacher and the child engage in two-way conversations to set goals that the child can accomplish while learning in the classroom.

- **Cross-curriculum teaching:** This is a teaching style in which individual subjects are not learned in isolation. Instead, the classroom is set up to encourage multitopic learning and larger units of study that encompass all the learning goals.

A teacher can benefit greatly from changing their teaching style to work best with the group of children currently in the classroom. This process will support the teacher in the long run, but the teacher may need increased support while making the change to something new and different. That is when an encouraging teaching team can step in to help. If an experienced teacher is accustomed to using certain materials or planning the same activities year after year, having a team of teachers working together can brainstorm new ideas and encourage one another to keep trying when a planned activity is unsuccessful.

ADEQUATE PLANNING TIME

Educators agree that planning time can be one of the largest factors to help support them in the classroom environment (Anderson, 2019). During the school day, teachers rarely have time to plan for the following week because they are spending most of their time interacting with children. In an inclusive classroom, many of those children may need one-on-one time with the teacher multiple times per day. With this demand for their time and attention, teachers are often forced to save their planning until all the children go home.

This means that teachers often plan and create lessons during their family time, at a child's sporting events, or when they are trying to relax at home in the evening while watching television. Not only does this cross the line of work-life balance, but it can cause teachers to burn out faster than other professions in which the employee gets to come home and forget about the job until the following day. Planning at home also means that the teacher may not be able to give their full attention to lesson planning, if they must multitask while doing it.

Administrators need to consider the teacher's time a precious commodity and focus it on the students and the curriculum development, instead of other activities that may take up time during the day. Of course, all staff members need their designated breaks, but there are other activities that could be removed from the teachers' responsibilities in order to show respect for their time. Tasks such as changing the toner in the copy machine or laminating materials for the classroom could be redirected to floating teachers or administrative staff. Having someone in the office who is designated as the technology expert can limit the amount of time that any one teacher struggles with a computer before asking for help. Also, allowing lead teachers to have a common planning time during the day creates a set time for lesson planning at work and a designated opportunity for brainstorming with other content experts who may be able to answer each other's questions.

OPPORTUNITIES FOR SELF-CARE

Teacher burnout is occurring at an alarming rate across the United States. Teachers are overworked and underpaid, but there are additional reasons that teachers are leaving the field (Sullivan, 2022):

- Poor classroom and program funding
- High emotional demands of the job
- Inadequate preparation and training programs
- Challenging teaching environments
- Larger classroom enrollment with no assistants

Many teachers don't initially identify that they are experiencing burnout. The symptoms are so bland that they can be attributed to many different causes. Some of the most common signs of teacher burnout include constant fatigue, lack of inspiration, self-doubt, and social withdrawal.

Administrators can help reduce teacher burnout by setting up polices in their programs to support teaching staff. These policies could include:

- Keeping open lines of communication between administrators and staff
- Planning activities specifically to boost staff morale
- Making sure that teachers feel trained to do the job they are assigned
- Allowing the whole staff to come together at times for staff meetings
- Finding ways to applaud staff for a job well done

Teachers also need to be proactive about taking care of themselves so that they do not experience burnout or even leave the field of teaching. Teachers need to maintain their own health by getting enough sleep, exercising, and eating a nutritious diet. They can also take care of themselves with the following strategies:

- Journaling
- Yoga
- Practicing reflection or mindfulness
- Counseling with a mental-health professional
- Breathing activities
- Positive affirmations
- Spending time in nature
- Taking naps
- Spending time with close friends

Whatever techniques the teacher decides to use, it is essential to devote time to herself or himself on occasion instead of constantly giving all their energy to others. Self-care can make it possible for the teacher to stay in the field much longer and serve many more children and families.

A Child-Care Teacher's Point of View

Marie is a certified early childhood educator with a great deal of experience in the field of early childhood special education. She has worked in both inclusive and noninclusive programs. One of her first jobs was at an inclusive child-care program that had pediatric therapists on staff to support children with a variety of disabilities. Marie left the field of early education for several years when her children were little, and when she returned, she was not able to obtain the same type of position that she had held before. For many early educators, working in an inclusive early childhood education program can offer as many benefits to the teachers, such as a reduction in classroom stress and receiving coaching from therapists, as it does for the children.

I have been teaching in the early childhood classroom for more than twenty years. I have a master's degree in interdisciplinary early childhood education, which includes special education, and I am certified as a developmental interventionist.

When I first started teaching, I was working with toddlers in an inclusive child-care program. I was the lead teacher in the classroom, and I had support from a physical therapist, speech pathologist, and an occupational therapist. I also had practicum students and student teachers. Sometimes, it felt like there were just as many adults in the classroom as there were toddlers, but when you are trying to support a room full of toddlers with and without disabilities, that is what you need.

The program in which I worked was amazing. When children seemed to have an "off day," the therapists would take them to the therapy swing to give them all the movement they needed until they calmed down. There were resources available for children in wheelchairs or walkers, and our speech pathologists did a wonderful job with both verbal and nonverbal children. Of course, we had only a few classrooms. Funding a large program with resources of that nature would have been extremely expensive. Also, every year we noticed a small amount of funding cuts, either from our government early intervention funding or from local funders like the United Way. There were lots of organizations that wanted to support initiatives like ours, but those funds are always coveted by many different organizations.

When my own children were little, I had the opportunity to stay home with them and leave the workforce for several years. When I re-entered, I went to work for a church child-care program where I knew the director, and I knew that she was striving to run a high-quality program. Again, I went to work with infants and toddlers because that really was my passion. I was now a veteran staff member compared to some of the newer employees. I was working with some women who were definitely career employees in the child-care field, but I was also working with some entry-level staff who thought a child-care program would be a good job while they went to college. To them, the position was a good fit because they didn't have to work nights and weekends. Because most of the full-time employees worked the early shifts, the younger employees loved working later in the day. Some of these men and women still work in child care and have learned how important it is to nurture young children, but others really only saw the job as a paycheck.

When you work with "paycheck employees" in a child-care program, it usually means that they try to maintain the status quo in the classroom until the parents arrive to pick up the children. There is a significant difference between the teaching staff who are there to interact with the children and the teaching staff who are there hoping that multiple children are out sick.

Teachers who don't put time and effort into developing relationships with the children often have classrooms where children are not well behaved. Those teachers then have to figure out what to do in response to the behavior problems. Less-trained teachers often end up resorting to putting children in time-out for every offense. That can be really challenging with toddlers and young preschoolers because they might not understand why they are in time-out. The infant room can be overwhelming for a teacher who thought that the only job was to rock babies. Even if only one child has colic or can't be soothed easily, then the whole classroom starts crying. A teacher who doesn't have a relationship with the infants doesn't know how to soothe the babies and just ends up bouncing babies up and down while begging them to stop crying.

Unfortunately, the babies who can't stop crying and the preschoolers who can't control their bodies usually include the children who have a developmental delay. We might not know what that delay is yet, but those children need the most help, not the most frustration. They need a relationship with the teachers so that they feel safe telling them what is wrong. They need a teacher who knows that they get gassy after having a bottle, so someone needs to burp them even longer. When a teacher doesn't spend the time developing that relationship with a child, the behavior never improves, and children never get what they need.

The one positive thing about the "paycheck employees" is that they don't last that long. They realize that caring for young children is a hard job, and they don't want to invest that much work in a part-time job. Teachers who are invested in working with young children and who learn the skills they need to work with children from different backgrounds are much more likely to stay in their jobs, but teachers who do not know how to support every child in the classroom do not end up being successful.

Eventually, the child-care program was under new management, and I ended up going back to the inclusive child-care program that I had worked for in the past. The program had changed quite a bit since I was there last. It was much larger; it now had fifteen classrooms. The program was still an inclusive program, but many people were enrolling their children because of the new location, not the mission statement of the program. Due to a continued lack of outside funding, the program had raised its tuition, so not every family who wanted to enroll their child due to a disability could afford the tuition. This was unfortunate, but child-care costs were rising everywhere, so it was somewhat expected.

The child-care program still had pediatric therapy at the facility, but the therapists were not as accessible as they had been previously. Health insurance billing had become so complicated that many of the therapists had to document every fifteen-minute increment that they spent with clients. The teachers still had the ability to ask for a therapy consult, and I was so grateful to see the therapists pop into my classroom to help. I just missed the old days when they could spend an extended amount of time with the children.

The whole class benefited when a therapist came in to do a session with a child. First, every child in the room was excited to see the therapist visit. I think parents are often apprehensive about letting their children see a therapist at school because they assume there is a stigma associated with the session. That is not the case in an early childhood classroom. Every other child is jealous when a therapist visits just one child. More often than not, the therapist interacts with multiple children because the patient needs to be in a social setting. This is always wonderful, in my opinion, because even typically developing children can benefit from this interaction. Sometimes the therapists even identify a child who might not be meeting a milestone in a certain area, and they give me a heads-up.

I was proud to be a part of a program that didn't punish children. When a young child demonstrated a negative behavior, our teachers interceded and redirected the child and told them what the positive behavior should be instead of just telling them no. The child-care program focused on helping all children in their classroom on their own developmental level, and the classroom numbers were small enough that it wasn't overwhelming to do that. I also loved walking into the classroom and not seeing behavior charts that display each child's behavior to the public.

Honestly, even when we had a new teacher who didn't have experience in an inclusive classroom start at the center, our policies set up the classroom for each child to learn individually. The staff members started with orientation designed by our education director, and then the new teachers had an opportunity to observe a veteran teacher to see how they run their classroom. The policies did not set that teacher up to discipline harshly. Instead, the redirection allowed children to receive instruction on what they should do instead of what they should not do. When the redirection did not work, then the therapists were there to offer additional guidance. If the therapists thought the child needed an evaluation or further support, then the teacher and the therapist would sit down with the family to make sure that everyone was on the same page and creating a unified plan to support the child.

Every child struggles at some point in time in the classroom. However, in this classroom setting, children did not lose playground time or sit in an isolated corner when they could not figure out how to follow the community rules. They were able to have a conversation with a teacher with whom they had a personal relationship. They were able to problem solve how to fix the situation that did not work. They were not shamed. Instead, they were told, "Do it this way instead."

All children need a break from other children and adults at times. Instead of time-out, children in this program were given the opportunity to have time to themselves. They were able to choose to have time alone because the classrooms offered quiet corners or areas that allow children to be alone. These areas were not the book corner, and they were not associated with a punishment.

Once children learned that they could choose to be alone when they needed the opportunity, and they realized that it was not a punishment, they began to use that part of the classroom frequently. Having that option helped them learn self-control and self-regulation in a positive manner. Children learn that being alone is not a punishment but something they occasionally need. When a child can choose alone time, then punishment can decrease, because negative interactions with peers can decrease. This option is not always afforded in a traditional preschool classroom. In most traditional classrooms, children are told where to be in the classroom and how to feel during a disagreement between themselves and a peer.

I think many child-care programs that are not designed to be inclusive believe that it will be very expensive to make accommodations for young children. That really isn't the case. A quiet corner can be a refrigerator box with pillows inside. The therapists often use simple accommodations for students. They used rolled-up towels to bolster a child's seating at circle time when the child may suffer from low muscle tone. They can use teethers or therapeutic tubing for children who are prone to biting or who have low mouth control. Children with poor fine-motor skills may need extra time playing with playdough or connecting blocks. These are materials most child-care programs already have, so there is no additional expense, only brainstorming.

There are families who feel defensive when a teacher suggests that they see some concerns with the child's development. I think the biggest difference in the inclusive classroom is that the teachers become more accustomed to talking to parents about this topic, and they learn ways to be more empathic before sharing overwhelming news. It is so important that teachers never tell parents what is wrong with a child, because it is easy for the teachers to be wrong.

Teachers in the inclusive classroom really need to rely on the data from developmental assessments and their observations about things with which the child is struggling in the classroom. If a teacher notices that a child struggles to interact with other children in the classroom, and the developmental assessment shows that the child is not meeting all of the social-emotional milestones, then it would be appropriate to share that information during a parent-teacher conference.

In a meeting with the parents, the teacher can give examples of when the child has struggled in the classroom. Then, the teacher can share possible ways that parents can support the child moving forward, such as speaking with a pediatrician or having an evaluation with a speech pathologist or occupational therapist. If the parents are defensive about the information, then the teacher can always assure the family that it is also an option to watch the child over time and see if the social and emotional skills progress. It is still appropriate to continue to share progress, or lack of progress, with the family over time so that the family members can continue to make informed decisions.

I now find myself in a traditional play-based preschool setting that is not focused on being inclusive but is focused on being a high-quality preschool program. When a program does not focus on inclusion, making it a priority, policies and procedures can end up targeting children with disabilities, whether or not that was the program's intent. I have an excellent director, but our higher leadership often makes decisions for our program based on financial constraints or on parent requests.

The biggest challenge working in a noninclusive center is that the curriculum is focused on the average ability of the children enrolled in the classroom. It is not designed to be individualized. In observing my coworkers, I notice that they are choosing activities that most children like. I don't want to condemn this practice, because it is common. If they don't have enough time or resources to spend time with every child in the classroom, then they plan their lessons to support as many children as possible and hope for the best. There is something to be said about exposing children to content and vocabulary that they are not yet ready to learn. Even if they aren't ready to learn it, at least they are being exposed to it. Ultimately, however, hoping to help as many students as possible is not the best way to teach. There must be a method where teachers interact purposefully with each individual child.

The inclusive classroom allows this to happen by avoiding the temptation to fill the physical space with the maximum number of children allowed. The inclusive program trains its teachers to practice teaching each individual student. That is a developed skill, and teachers must have training on it to be successful. Most child-care training programs train teachers on how to create a lesson plan, but many programs do not show teachers how to modify that lesson plan so that it applies to all students.

I am still teaching in a toddler classroom, so the greatest behavior struggles each day involve the children biting one another. My current child-care program was more forgiving of biting in the past, but due to continuous parent complaints, we have had to implement a biting policy. The new policy has more severe consequences for children who are frequent biters. As soon as the policy was enacted, I had one family who voiced how scared they were about the child biting and losing a spot in the toddler room.

They won't be the only family who is scared. Every year I have at least one child in my classroom who is a biter. Of course, some of those children struggle with biting more than others do. Some have a problem with biting because it is a learned behavior, but others struggle because biting is a sign of a bigger problem. It could be a child struggling with sensory issues. It could be a child with a language delay that is using biting to communicate with peers. It could be a child with a social or emotional delay that does not know how to communicate effectively with others. If there is a blanket policy on biting, children with disabilities will be at a disadvantage.

The other problem with a biting policy is that it ultimately leads to suspension or expulsion. This can be devasting to all families. Parents need child care so that they go to work, and when they are in danger of losing their child care, that can also endanger the family's income and stability.

Because losing child care can have such negative consequences, parents react strongly when they read these types of policies.

In my years of working in child-care programs, it seems that suspension and expulsion hurt families more than any other process. It also seems that children with disabilities are more likely to be expelled when policies don't support the children and families. If a child doesn't fit the mold that a child-care program wants, then they are at risk of expulsion. Child-care programs are not as direct as elementary and secondary schools when it comes to expulsion. The child-care programs talk more about insurance liability and lack of staffing. They tell the parents that they just can't take proper care of the child, and then they tell the family to find somewhere else for the child to go to school.

I understand that private child-care programs don't get special-education money. I also understand that some centers must have as many students as possible in a classroom to survive financially, and that those adult-to-child ratios don't really support children with disabilities. Yet, I wonder whether the child-care program actually attempted classroom accommodations before they told the parents to find other child care. With a child who is biting, did they try to use a vibrating teething ring or an ice pop? Did they allow for flexible seating at circle time and shorten the length of time that children were required to pay attention? Or did they just decide that the child cannot follow the exact same directions that the other students follow, so that child needs to find a new child-care setting. Maybe it is just easier for some child-care programs to dismiss students that cause problems, especially if they have a waitlist of other students that can immediately fill that spot.

My job as an early childhood educator is to serve all the children in my classroom, not just the children who easily follow directions and comply with the classroom rules. In fact, the children who do not follow the rules need my help even more than the others do. Someone still has to show them how to explore the environment and learn how to problem solve, even if they communicate with a friend by hitting. Someone has to help the toddlers learn how to share their toys, even when they bite a friend. All children are special and unique, and every child needs love and attention regardless of their individual differences.

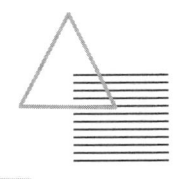

CHAPTER 8

Collaboration and Inclusion

A teacher holds an extremely important role in the life of a young child; however, for the teacher to be as successful as possible, they must collaborate with other key individuals in the child's life. All teachers must strive to partner with the children's families to create the greatest level of consistency between home and school. This partnership should influence both environments: the family influences how the teacher relates to the child in the classroom setting, and the teacher supports the family with developmentally appropriate strategies that can be used at home. Without this key relationship in place, it is difficult to provide a child with the best possible early childhood education.

Key community partners also benefit the child-care program and, therefore, improve the quality of education in the inclusive classroom. One vital partnership is the local public school system. This relationship is essential when the child-care program and the public school system have a contract in place to care for the same children; however, the relationship is still essential when the two organizations are not contract partners. Ultimately, most of the children enrolled in the child-care program will transition from the inclusive child-care classroom to public school kindergarten. To prepare children for the public school system, your child-care center must understand how public school policies work and what the educational expectations will be for children enrolled in the program.

Inclusive child-care programs should also partner with other community organizations to provide supports to the inclusive classroom. State-funded early intervention programs and private pediatric therapy practices can be key partners to offer on-site therapy to students who do not qualify for therapy in the public school system. Many child-care programs may also partner with local pediatricians or the local health department to receive trainings on how to support medically fragile children. Local child care advocacy groups that specifically support one type of disability and provide those families with support groups, family activities, and local resources can also partner with child-care programs.

The most important part of collaboration with family and community partners is to make sure that everyone at the table has the same priorities:

- Valuing each individual child and their differences
- Valuing everyone's unique contribution to that child's life
- Trusting one another to work in the best interest of the child
- Dedicating time and effort to professional communication between organizations
- Making decisions together for a mutually agreeable partnership

FAMILIES

Family-teacher collaboration can be successful when the foundation of the relationship is a sense of equity. At no time should an educator speak down to a parent or scold them for what the teacher believes are improper strategies to support the child. Educators must remember that the family member is the expert on the child. Although teachers will spend a concentrated amount of time with the child during the course of one school year, the family is with the child for a lifetime. Families do not feel comfortable partnering with a teacher or director who patronizes them or shames them for improper parenting. The one exception to this rule is if the educator or other staff member believes that a child is being abused or neglected. Educators are mandatory reporters and must contact Child Protective Services if they suspect a child is being harmed.

Many relationships between teachers and family members may begin by feeling awkward or stiff. The goal is to create sincere relationships, so teachers need to go out of their way to start genuine conversations and ask how the families are doing. Teachers should remain open-minded about the family's values and priorities. The teacher may not agree with the parenting strategies being used in the home, but if the family is functioning in a healthy way, then it is up to the family members to decide what works in their own home.

The purpose of creating a relationship with the family is to make it easier for the family to share information about what is happening in the child's life. This information, in turn, makes it easier to support the child in the classroom and to contact the family—if needed—to problem solve challenging situations. The family is more likely to work with a teacher to find a solution if trust has already been established.

Education

A large part of family collaboration can be the child-care program's efforts to increase family education. Not all parents have a skill set surrounding child development and early education, so they may have questions about the materials in the classroom, what skills the materials are teaching, and the timeline for children to learn certain developmental skills. This is an area in which teachers can support parents by providing information. Many family members are just learning about how teachers can support children with disabilities in the classroom. They need information about ways to help calm their children down when they can't regulate their bodies or emotions. Other family members may need information about what type of play activities they can do with their children at home to help develop the child's fine- and gross-motor skills. Providing parent education can help family members feel more confident interacting with their children and can help them learn how to advocate for their children. Child-care programs can offer this type of support to families through

- parent education nights,
- digital handouts,
- newsletters,
- blogs or the center website,
- displays in the child-care program or in the classroom, and
- parent-teacher conferences.

Be proactive about offering this information so that families will be less likely to come to your program with concerns about why the child is "playing" all day in the classroom instead of learning.

Teach family members about the importance of their involvement in a child's education. The kindergarten through twelfth-grade education system will not encourage parents to be as involved as the early childhood program will, but it is essential for a family to be involved throughout their child's education journey. If your child-care program encourages involvement when the child is young and helps the parents create these habits, then they will have established partnerships that can last throughout a child's educational experience. The school can focus on emphasizing the following topics to parents and caregivers:

- Setting appropriate academic goals for your child
- How parent involvement affects the child's overall performance
- How to help a child develop positive classroom behavior
- Creating a positive learning environment at home
- Creating a year-round learning environment when school is not in session

Family-Teacher Communication and Conferences

Most child-care programs have established systems of communication so families know when and how to expect communication and where to find answers to their questions. Some of the most common forms of communication between child-care programs and families include the following:

- a communication app for the center,
- a weekly educational blog or monthly center newsletter,
- an email listserv,
- postings in the center or the classroom,
- personal conversations during daily drop-off and pick-up time,
- program open-house nights, and
- parent-teacher conferences.

Communication should not be so frequent that families are overwhelmed and stop reading center emails or newsletters. Instead, communication should occur at predictable intervals, unless there is a situation that needs immediate attention. Weekly classroom emails and monthly center newsletters can be excellent ways to share information without demanding too much of the families' time.

In an inclusive child-care program, the family-teacher conference gives teachers the opportunity to discuss the child's overall development in the classroom setting, learn what the parents' goals are for the child, discuss the child's developmental assessment with the family, and discuss interventions or enrichments being used in the classroom to support the child. During these conferences, teachers may also share concerns with the family about a child who is not meeting their developmental milestones. Although these conversations can be challenging for the teacher to have and tough for the family to hear, a teacher's preparation goes a long way to making these conversations positive and productive.

Before a teacher ever sits down to talk with a parent, it is important that the teacher does some homework. Make sure to know the likes and dislikes of the child, the results of the child's developmental assessments, and background information about the family. Start the conversation with positive information, such as what the child enjoys doing at school and areas of development in which the child has grown during the current school year. Share the child's artwork or pictures of the child interacting in the classroom.

Before beginning a discussion on developmental milestones, have all the necessary information ready and available. Share the results from any developmental assessments, provide work samples, and share notes from classroom observations. Avoid using jargon or "teacher talk." Share all information in plain language. Ask questions and listen carefully to the family. Be prepared to answer their questions. Listen to the family's concerns about the child. Ask how the family how they successfully calm the child down in the home, and ask whether the child demonstrates concerning behaviors at home. If you are sharing negative news about a child's development or performance in the classroom, be prepared for the family to rebut with criticism of you as the educator. It is important to have a thick skin and understand that the news may be painful for the family to hear. Be empathetic. Remember that, as an educator, you view children differently from the way the parents do. When you share information about a child with the family, you may need to give several examples in different scenarios, so that the parents can begin to understand your concern.

After the conference, follow up by thanking the family member for attending and asking if there are any additional questions. Keep the lines of communication open so that the family members feel comfortable asking questions once they have had time to process all the information you shared with them. Some family members may go through stages of acceptance, almost like the stages of grief, in which they process that their child may have a developmental delay. Balance the time the family needs to cope with this information against the necessity of moving forward to get the child necessary supports.

Medical Emergency Plans

When a child enrolled in a child-care program has a medical condition that may require emergency medical treatment, child-care staff and the family must sit down together to discuss what needs to happen during an emergency. Parents need to share information on emergency medication, whether or not to call 911, how to support the child after the emergency, and other essential topics.

Most medical emergency plans in child-care programs deal with asthma attacks, allergic reactions, seizures, or dramatic changes in blood sugar. In most of these cases, the family will already know the child's diagnosis and have a specific preference on how to treat the child. Emergency medication may need to be kept at the child-care program in a secure site where teachers know how to access it. The administrative staff will need to make sure that all staff members who work with the child are trained on the child's medical needs. Parents will need to be sure to update the medical plan with the child-care program whenever the treating physician makes adjustments to the child's care.

Special-Education Meetings

Special-education meetings are hosted by the public school system. For children who are older than three years, a committee reviews the results of a child's developmental evaluation and determines whether the child needs an IEP. The state-funded early intervention program will host special-education meetings to determine whether a child under the age of three years needs an IFSP to receive early intervention therapy. These meetings typically consist of the family, the caseworker from the state organization, the diagnostician who evaluated the child, the therapists who could be serving the child on the new plan, and the classroom teacher or developmental interventionist.

If the child attends an inclusive, private child-care program, the parents still have the opportunity to invite the program teacher or the director to be a part of the meeting. The family has the right to invite a specialist in the field who is knowledgeable about the child. If the child-care program has a partnership with the public school system, then the teacher at the program may be the teacher who is invited to the meeting. The primary job of the teacher in this meeting is to speak up for the rights of the child and fight for all the support services that the child may need to be successful.

These meetings can be emotional and difficult for the family, so someone on the committee needs to help the family remember all the ways that the child is special. The child's teacher can remind the family of all of the child's skills and successes, instead of allowing them to sit through a two-hour meeting where the focus is on the child's deficits.

COMMUNITY

When a child-care program partners with the community, that can mean partnering with public or private entities that will help support the children enrolled in the program. Some partnerships are not extensive. For example, a partner organization might come to the child-care program once or twice a year to share resources. Other partnerships, such as one with the public school system, could be much more extensive and even require a contract outlining what each partner will bring to the agreement. Learn about the resources that are available in your community and region so that the children at your program can receive the best resources possible.

Public School System

There are two primary types of partnerships that a child-care program can have with the public school system. In the first type, the child-care program reaches out for information about family events and kindergarten enrollment to share with enrolled families. The child-care program stays updated on kindergarten screenings and academic standards to make sure to help all students be as prepared for kindergarten as possible. This is a low-involvement partnership, but it is still essential to obtain all the necessary information for enrolled families.

The second type of partnership for a child-care program and the public school system is usually a contractual partnership in which the school system will send certain students to the inclusive child-care program when they do not have available space in the local school district's public school preschool classrooms. The public school will typically give the child-care program a stipend per child to pay for the cost of education for the children, but the public school will still provide the needed therapies required by the child's IEP. In this type of partnership, the child-care program must meet the minimum standards of quality required by the school system in order to continue receiving funds. This model can be extremely helpful to both partners. The child-care program receives enrollment and funding for each child, and the public school system does not have the capital expense of adding classrooms or trying to find additional staffing. This model is also helpful to parents who need full-time, year-round care instead of just school-day hours. Several states such as Georgia and West Virginia have used this model for their universal prekindergarten programs, and they have been successful.

IDEA Part C Services

Disability services through IDEA Part C involve early intervention for children from birth until age three. These services are available in all states, but this is not full-time child-care enrollment like the public school preschool. The enrollment is limited to the pediatric therapies that are included in the child's IFSP. The goal of IDEA Part C services is to offer children their therapy in their natural environment. For children who attend full-time child care, their inclusive child-care classroom is their natural environment. The child-care program would partner with the IDEA Part C therapists to allow the specialists to come into their program to work with the infants and toddlers in their classroom setting.

This partnership can be helpful for both the parents and the child-care program. First, many parents have a hard time setting up these appointments, leaving work during the day, and taking their children to therapy. When the therapist comes to child care, it takes one more burden off of the family's plate. Having a therapist in the classroom is also beneficial for the child-care program, because the teachers can see the interventions that the therapists are using with the children and learn how to use them in the classroom when the therapists are not there. This in itself can be in-depth training on special education.

Private Therapy Practices

Partnering with private therapy practices can be similar to partnering with IDEA Part C services. Children who receive therapy from an outside organization can have those therapists attend the child-care program to offer children individualized therapy in the child's natural setting. Another option is for the child-care program to partner with the pediatric therapy practice to work with children on-site for a set number of days a week and do developmental evaluations as needed. This partnership may involve the pediatric therapy practice coming to the child-care program one day to conduct screenings for all children whose families sign a release. For the children who show red flags on the initial screening, the pediatric practice can reach out to the family about how to proceed. The therapy practice can bill the families' health insurance for a full evaluation and, if the child qualifies for therapy, the therapist can come back to the child-care program to offer services. In cases where multiple children at one center qualify for and request regular therapy services, the pediatric practice may reserve time each week to visit the child-care program to offer therapy. This would be cheaper for the child-care program than hiring its own therapy staff, but it would still give teachers access to therapists when challenging behaviors arise and offer families the option of on-site evaluations.

Family Support Groups

Family support groups for certain disability populations can be a huge asset for an inclusive child-care program. They often have prepared presentations that they can provide on family education nights that can give parents more information on specific disabilities, the special-education system, or long-term financial planning for families with disabled children. Many of these organizations have annual events such as 5K walks and awareness nights in the community. Connecting currently enrolled families with these groups can help the parents find people who are going through the same emotions as they are and who can offer support. They can also give families an opportunity to learn more about the disability and connect their children with other children who may have a similar diagnosis. Sometimes, one of the greatest resources for the families we work with is to meet someone else experiencing a similar situation.

Community Advocacy Groups

Most communities have some type of childhood advocacy organization that fights for the rights of young children at the local, state, or federal level. Many policies in school systems, in doctors' offices, and with health insurance companies are not supportive of families who have a child with a disability. An advocacy group has paid or volunteer lobbyists who will fight for those families at the local level or even up to the national level so that children have every opportunity to have happy and productive lives. Some advocacy efforts may start in small parent groups that focus on specific disabilities, but there are also larger advocacy organizations that work at a much larger level, such as the Autism Society of America or the National Down Syndrome Congress.

Child-care programs have not always done a good job advocating for themselves and their policies, so it may not be a natural partnership for them to turn to a child advocacy organization. The key is for the staff members to remember that they have a personal story and so do the families. Those personal stories, shared with the right elected officials, can make a huge impact on behalf of many different children with disabilities. Your child-care staff does not have to become part of the advocacy work, but it is important to have a partnership with these types of agencies to help parents know where to turn for support. In an inclusive child-care setting, your staff is guiding both the children and their families.

These efforts to collaborate with families and community organizations will all support a program-wide effort for accommodations for children with disabilities. Supporting children with disabilities and watching typically developing children thrive in an inclusive environment are the major goals for inclusive child-care programs. If a classroom supports children with disabilities, then it will support all the children who learn there.

Many children are struggling to find quality child care. Children with disabilities cannot get what they need to be successful in just any child-care program. An inclusive child-care program can allow any and every child to be successful if it follows best practice and individualizes the education for all children enrolled. Programs considering a transition to an inclusive child-care environment will be meeting the needs of all children, which is the reason that most early childhood educators enter the field to begin with: to care for and educate all children.

APPENDIX
Child-Care Self-Evaluation for Inclusive Programs

This evaluation tool is based on the ten accreditation standards of the National Association for the Education of Young Children (n.d.) for high-quality early childhood programs. Each component should be ranked: *consistently, sometimes,* or *never*. This survey will indicate the areas of the child-care program that need additional support to be fully inclusive and to prepare all children to be successful in kindergarten.

Standard I: Relationships	Consistently	Sometimes	Never
Caregivers are with the same children each day.			
The classroom offers a language-rich environment.			
Teachers spend time in back-and-forth conversations with children each day.			
The classroom setting encourages positive behaviors and group play.			
Teachers help children identify emotions and involve children in conflict resolution.			
Teachers participate in play with children to model appropriate use of materials and encourage conversation during play.			
Teachers and administrators have collaborative staff meetings to encourage morale and work toward an inclusive mission.			
The program establishes events to invite families into the classroom and get to know staff.			

Standard II: Curriculum	Consistently	Sometimes	Never
The classroom uses developmentally appropriate curriculum based on the children's developmental milestones, not just themes or the age of the children.			
The program uses a play-based curriculum with open-ended materials so that children can explore instead of being told what to do with the classroom tools.			
The curriculum addresses the following content areas:			
Fine-motor development			
Large-motor development			
Art			
Music and movement			
Dramatic play			
Block play			
Nature and science			
Math			
Language and literacy			
Technology			
Cultural diversity			

Standard III: Teaching	Consistently	Sometimes	Never
Teachers offer individualized lessons and small-group learning opportunities whenever possible.			
Teachers offer large-group lessons, but children have the option not to participate in the large group.			
The staff are responsive to children's needs and vary teaching strategies as needed.			
Teachers offer play-based learning with ample opportunities for exploration.			
Teachers offer process-based art activities instead of structured craft projects.			

Standard IV: Assessment of Child Progress	Consistently	Sometimes	Never
The program offers two or more developmental screenings per year, to watch and monitor the children's progress.			
The program obtains consent from the families before completing screenings/assessments.			
Teachers administering the screenings/assessments have been trained on how to use the tools.			
Teachers use the data from the completed assessments to set individual goals for the children.			
Teachers share the data from the completed assessments with the families and explain what the results mean.			
The screenings/assessments used cover multiple developmental domains.			
Teachers use authentic assessments that allow them to observe the children completing the skills in the classroom during play.			
The screenings/assessments are culturally appropriate for the children enrolled in the classroom.			

Standard V: Health	Consistently	Sometimes	Never
The classroom offers a low adult-to-child ratio.			
The program has safety procedures for administering medication.			
The staff members are trained on first aid and CPR.			
The program has policies for protecting children with food allergies, and staff members are trained on how to use an EpiPen.			
All staff members, regular volunteers, and regular visitors have extensive background checks in place.			
The program has emergency plans for children with severe health conditions, such as epilepsy, diabetes, and so on.			
The classroom is set up so that children can be independent when washing their hands, toileting, and feeding themselves.			

Standard VI: Staff Competencies, Preparation, and Support	Consistently	Sometimes	Never
Lead teachers possess degrees or certifications in child development, early childhood education, or special education.			
Teaching staff have experience working with children with different abilities and health concerns.			
The program offers the staff members annual training on some aspect of inclusive classrooms.			
The program administrator supervises professional growth plans for all staff, to assist with developing essential skills.			
The program offers planning time to the teachers so they can create inclusive lesson plans.			
The staff have paid time off for illness and personal leave.			
The administration plans activities and incentives to support staff morale.			

Standard VII: Relationships	Consistently	Sometimes	Never
The program has an open-door policy for families of enrolled children.			
The program sets up communication systems for teachers and administrators to communicate with families: website, social media, emails, apps, newsletters, daily sheets, and so on.			
The administrator and the teachers are able to meet with a family at their request.			
The program has regularly scheduled parent-teacher conferences.			
The program offers parent education workshops or events.			
The families are involved in decision-making for their children.			
The families are referred to outside professionals when they are needed.			

Standard VIII: Community Relationships	Consistently	Sometimes	Never
The program has compiled a list of community resources to share with families.			
The program collaborates with community pediatric therapy offices and local health departments to offer services on-site as needed.			
The program collaborates with local public schools to help children successfully transition to kindergarten.			
The program partners with local child-care resource and referral agencies to help direct children toward inclusive child care.			
The program partners with local colleges and trade schools to provide practicum students and student teachers as additional support in the classrooms and to offer training to students.			
The program collaborates with community parents' groups, such as the Down Syndrome Society and Autism Awareness, to use their resources.			

Standard IX: Physical Environment	Consistently	Sometimes	Never
The classrooms have ample indoor space for moving (including moving with assistive devices).			
The classrooms have child-sized furniture that are sized appropriately for the age of the children enrolled.			
The classroom has surfaces that are easy to clean.			
The classroom has storage space to put away materials when needed.			
The classroom has a cozy area.			
The classroom has an area that allows a child to be alone if needed.			
The playground surface is even to assist with mobility.			
The facility has a wheelchair ramp.			
The preschool classrooms have an area for diapering.			
The classroom has an adaptive toilet and sink for children with physical disabilities.			
The classroom has an area for large-group activities and space for small-group learning.			
The facility has a physical space for private parent-teacher conferences.			

Standard X: Leadership and Management	Consistently	Sometimes	Never
The program has a vision statement and mission to serve children of all abilities.			
The program has community partnerships that allow pediatric therapists to come in the building to work with children enrolled in the child-care program (with family permission).			
The program holds staff accountable for professional-development plans and annual goals.			
The program selects school-wide curriculum and assessments that support children of all abilities.			
The program supports staff members with planning time, breaks, and paid time off from work.			
The program manages staffing so that classrooms with more challenging behavior needs have additional staff support when needed.			

REFERENCES AND RECOMMENDED READING

20 USC 1400. 2004. Individuals with Disabilities Education Improvement Act of 2004.

Anderson, Jill. 2019. "The Gift of Teacher Time." Usable Knowledge, Harvard Graduate School of Education. https://www.gse.harvard.edu/news/uk/19/09/gift-teacher-time

Bishop, Sandra. 2023. *$122 Billion: The Growing, Annual Cost of the Infant-Toddler Child Care Crisis.* Ready Nation. https://strongnation.s3.amazonaws.com/documents/1598/05d917e2-9618-4648-a0ee-1b35d17e2a4d.pdf?1674854626&inline;%20filename=%22%24122%20Billion:%20The%20Growing,%20Annual%20Cost%20of%20the%20Infant-Toddler%20Child%20Care%20Crisis.pdf%22

Brown, Lydia. 2022. "Identity-First Language." Autistic Self Advocacy Network. https://autisticadvocacy.org/about-asan/identity-first-language/

Bullock, Greg. 2017. "Photosensitive Epilepsy: How Light Can Trigger Seizures." Theraspecs. https://www.theraspecs.com/blog/photosensitive-epilepsy-how-different-types-of-light-can-trigger-seizures/

Center for Applied Special Technology. 2022. "Universal Design for Learning Guidelines." CAST. https://www.cast.org/impact/universal-design-for-learning-udl

Centers for Disease Control and Prevention. 2022. "Health Insurance Portability and Accountability Act of 1996 (HIPAA)." CDC. https://www.cdc.gov/phlp/publications/topic/hipaa.html

Centers for Disease Control and Prevention. 2022. "Increase in Developmental Disabilities for Children in the United States." CDC. https://www.cdc.gov/ncbddd/developmentaldisabilities/features/increase-in-developmental-disabilities.html

DEC/NAEYC. 2009. *Early Childhood Inclusion: A Joint Position Statement of the Division for Early Childhood (DEC) and the National Association for the Education of Young Children (NAEYC).* Chapel Hill: The University of North Carolina, FPG Child Development Institute.

Easterseals. 2022. "Disability Etiquette." Easterseals. https://www.easterseals.com/support-and-education/facts-about-disability/disability-etiquette.html

Extension Alliance for Better Child Care. 2019. "What Is Inclusive Child Care?" Extension Alliance for Better Child Care. https://childcare.extension.org/what-is-inclusive-child-care/

Fang, Zuyi, et al. 2022. "Global Estimates of Violence against Children with Disabilities: An Updated Systematic Review and Meta-Analysis." *The Lancet Child and Adolescent Health* 6(5): P313–P323. https://doi.org/10.1016/S2352-4642(22)00033-5

Harms, Thelma, Richard M. Clifford, and Debby Cryer. 2014. *Early Childhood Environment Rating Scale*. 3rd edition. New York: Teachers College Press.

Harms, Thelma, Debby Cryer, Richard M. Clifford, and Noreen Yazejian. 2017. *Infant/Toddler Environment Rating Scale*. 3rd edition. New York: Teachers College Press.

Johnson, David W., and Roger T. Johnson. 2023. "Overview of Cooperative Learning." Cooperative Learning Institute. http://www.co-operation.org/what-is-cooperative-learning

Meek, Shantel E., and Walter S. Gilliam. 2016. "Expulsion and Suspension in Early Education as Matters of Social Justice and Health Equity." Perspectives. https://cca-ct.org/wp-content/uploads/2020/11/Expulsion-and-Suspension-in-Early-Education-as-Matters-of-Social-Justice-and-Health-Equity.pdf

National Association for the Education of Young Children. n.d. "The 10 NAEYC Program Standards." NAEYC. https://www.naeyc.org/our-work/families/10-naeyc-program-standards

National Association for the Education for Young Children. 2023. "Understanding and Responding to Children Who Bite." NAEYC. https://www.naeyc.org/our-work/families/understanding-and-responding-children-who-bite

National Institute of Neurological Disorders and Stroke. 2023. "Febrile Seizures." National Institute of Health. https://www.ninds.nih.gov/health-information/disorders/febrile-seizures#:~:text=Febrile%20seizures%20are%20seizures%20or,flu%2C%20or%20an%20ear%20infection

Novoa, Cristina. 2020. "The Child Care Crisis Disproportionately Affects Children with Disabilities." Center for American Progress. https://www.americanprogress.org/article/child-care-crisis-disproportionately-affects-children-disabilities

Shapiro, Anna, and Daphna Bassok. 2022. "Supporting Young Children with Disabilities during the COVID-19 Pandemic: Evidence from Caregivers in Virginia." AERA Open. https://journals.sagepub.com/doi/10.1177/23328584221134525

Springbrook Autism Behavioral Health. 2017. "Heavy Work: A Beneficial Occupational Therapy for Autism." Springbrook Autism Behavioral Health. https://springbrookbehavioral.com/heavy-work-a-beneficial-occupational-therapy-for-autism/

Sullivan, Emily T. 2022. "An Early Childhood Director Fears the Worst for the Field—and Wonders If Anyone Will Save It." EdSurge. https://www.edsurge.com/news/2022-12-06-an-early-childhood-director-fears-the-worst-for-the-field-and-wonders-if-anyone-will-save-it

US Department of Education. n.d.a. "Individuals with Disabilities Education Act." IDEA. https://sites.ed.gov/idea

US Department of Education. n.d.b. "Statute and Regulations." IDEA. https://sites.ed.gov/idea/statuteregulations/#regulations

US Department of Health and Human Services, Office for Civil Rights. 2006. "Your Rights Under Section 504 of the Rehabilitation Act." Fact Sheet. https://www.hhs.gov/sites/default/files/ocr/civilrights/resources/factsheets/504.pdf

US Department of Labor. 2022. "Americans with Disabilities Act." US Department of Labor. https://www.dol.gov/general/topic/disability/ada

Wood, Sarah. 2022. "What Is Differentiated Instruction?" *US News and World Report*. October 22. https://www.usnews.com/education/k12/articles/what-is-differentiated-instruction

Young, Natalie A. E., and Katrina Crankshaw. 2021. "Disability Rates Highest Among American Indian and Alaska Native Children and Children Living in Poverty." US Census Bureau. https://www.census.gov/library/stories/2021/03/united-states-childhood-disability-rate-up-in-2019-from-2008.html

INDEX

504 plans, 32–33

A

Accessibility of facilities and programs, 4–5, 76–78
Accommodations, 76–89
    behavior-management, 80–83
    classroom materials, 78–79
    curriculum, 80
    facility accommodations, 76–78
    meals, 83–84
Accreditation programs, 52–53
Adult-to-child ratios, 31, 38, 59, 63, 74, 93
Advocacy groups, 115–116
Aggressive behaviors, 60–62, 73, 105–106
Allergies, 83–84
Americans with Disabilities Act (ADA), 28–29
Author's experiences
    with medical diagnosis, v–vii
    as mother, x–xiv
    as new preschool teacher, vii–x

B

Behavior charts, 86
Behavior management policies, 71–73, 80–83
    behaviors, negative, 60–62, 73, 105–106
Biting, 60–62, 73, 105–106
Braille, 50
Burnout, 98–99

C

Camera systems, closed-circuit, 68
Caseworkers, 94
Child abuse/neglect, 108

Child Find, 31
Child Protective Services, 108
Children
    benefits of inclusive child care, 8–11
    benefits of inclusive child care for typically developing children, 13–14, 45, 49–50
    identification of children with disabilities, 31
Circle time, 20–22, 25, 86–87, 88–89, 106
Classroom materials, 78–79
Classroom observation, 68
Closed-circuit camera systems, 68
Collaboration and inclusion, 107–116
    community level, 113–116
    family-teacher collaboration, 108–112
Community advocacy groups, 115–116
Confidentiality of records, 32, 67–68
    under HIPAA, 33
Cooperative learning, 96
Cost and funding issues, 28, 59–60, 63
COVID-19 pandemic, 2
Cross-curriculum teaching, 97
Curriculum, 71, 80
Curriculum-based assessments, 95

D

Developmental assessments, 95–96
Developmental delay, definitions and overview, 1–2
Developmental milestones, 1, 95
    family communication regarding, 110–111
Differentiated learning, 97
Director's perspective vignette, mixed-delivery program, 44–51
Disability, definitions and overview, 1–2
Discipline and guidance, 75, 87–88
Discrimination, laws preventing, 27–29, 32–33
Due-process hearings, 33–34

E

Early Childhood Environment Rating Scale, 73
Early Steps early intervention program, 85–86
Emergency drills, 70
Employee handbooks. *See* Staff and family handbooks
Engagement (UDL component), 6–7
Enrollment procedures, 58
Etiquette of respect, 8
Expectations, appropriate, 83
Expression (UDL component), 6
Expulsion and suspension policies, 49, 60–61, 63–64, 71–72, 105–106

F

Families
    benefits of inclusive child care, 11–12
    family education, 109–110
    family education events, 50
    family observation/involvement, 50
    family support groups, 115
    family-teacher collaboration, 108–112
    family-teacher communication and conferences, 62, 104, 110–111
    transition to public school settings, 50
Family Educational Rights and Privacy Act (FERPA), 32, 67
Feeding therapy, 46, 83
First person narratives. *See* vignettes
Floating teachers, 93–94, 98
Free and appropriate public education (FAPE), 29, 31
    due-process hearings, 33–34
Friendships, 14. *See also* Peer support/role models
Furniture, classroom, 77–78

G

Goal-setting
    for child-care centers, 53–54
    for children, as teaching strategy, 97
    long-term goals for child-care centers, 42–44
    for teaching staff, 92–93

H

Health and safety requirements, 70–71

HIPAA (Health Insurance Portability and Accountability Act), 33, 67

I

Inclusive classrooms
- benefits for child-care programs, 12–15
- benefits for children, 8–11
- benefits for families, 11–12
- characteristics of, 4–8

Individual education plans (IEPs), 5, 10, 30, 32, 94, 96, 112

Individual family service plans (IFSPs), 5, 10, 30, 32, 96, 112

Individuals with Disabilities Education Improvement Act (IDEA), 29–32, 45
- Part C services, 114

Infant/Toddler Environment Rating Scale, 73

Instruction. *see* Curriculum; Teaching styles

Interdisciplinary early childhood education (IECE), 46

J

Job descriptions, 74

L

Language
- children's vocabulary, xi, 89, 105
- inappropriate, from parents, 64
- language skills, limited, and aggression, 60–61, 105
- people-first vs. identity-first language, 7
- sign language, 80

Laws surrounding special education. *See* Special education laws

Least restrictive environment (LRE), x, 30

Lighting, 78

M

Mandatory reporters, 108

Mealtime accommodations, 83–84

Medical emergency plans, 111–112

Mentors for new teachers, 91

Mission statements, 37–44
- components of, 37–38
- long-term goals, 42–43
- program values, 40–42
- sample, 38–39
- timelines for goals, 43–44
- writing process, 39–40

Mixed-delivery systems, 31–32
- director's perspective vignette, 44–51

Montessori, Maria, 13

Movement breaks, 80–81

N

National Association for the Education of Young Children, 52–53
- NAEYC standards, 53–54
- NAEYC standards self-evaluation, 117–126

Negative behaviors, 60–62, 71–73, 102

Noise levels, 79

O

Occupational therapy vignette, 84–89. *See also* Therapists in the classroom

One-on-one support, 47, 63, 81, 83, 87, 97

Open-door policies, 50

P

Parent's perspective vignette, 15–26

Participation, encouragement of, 5

Peer support/role models, 9–10, 13, 45, 51, 81–82

People First Respectful Language Modernization Act, 7

People-first vs. identity-first language, 7

Planning time for teachers, 53, 97–98

Play-based learning, 87

Playgrounds, 77

Policy-setting, 57–75
- challenging behaviors, 60–62
- classroom observations, 68
- confidentiality, 67–68

    cost, 59–60
    enrollment procedures, 58
    program visitors, 64–66
    staff and family handbooks, 69–75
    suspension and expulsion, 63–64
Positive feedback, 82
Positive redirection, 72, 75, 87–88
Privacy. *See* Confidentiality of records
Professional development for teachers, 91–93
Program operations, 74
Program visitors, 64–66
Progress, documentation of, 5
Public-private partnerships, 31
Public school system partnerships, 113
Punishment, avoiding, 102–103

Q
Quiet corners, 103

R
Redirection, positive, 72, 75, 87–88
Rehabilitation Act, Section 504, 32–33
Representation (UDL component), 6
Respect
    etiquette of, 8
    and social/emotional skills for children, 13–14
Routines, consistent, 82

S
Safety
    and aggressive behaviors, 60–62
    health and safety requirements, 70–71
    medical emergency plans, 111–112
    playground accommodations, 77
    and program visitors, 64–66
Schedules, 82
Screening and evaluation

screening processes, 46, 58

screening tools, 95

Self-assessment for child-care centers, 52–53

self-evaluation checklist, 117–126

Self-care for teachers, 98–99

Sign language, 80

Social interactions. *See* Peer support/role models

Special-education coordinators, 94

Special education laws, 27–34

Americans with Disabilities Act (ADA), 28–29

due-process hearings, 33–34

HIPAA, 33

Individuals with Disabilities Education Improvement Act (IDEA), 29–32

Section 504 of the Rehabilitation Act, 32–33

Special-education meetings, 112

Staff and family handbooks, 57, 69–75

behavior-management policies, 71–73

curriculum, 71

discipline and guidance, 75

health and safety requirements, 70–71

job descriptions, 74

mission and vision, 69–70

program operations, 74

Staffing

funding issues, 51

staff education, 47–48

support staff, 94

See also Teaching staff

Stress and burnout

parents and caregivers, 11

self-care for teachers, 98–99

Student observers/practicum teachers, 65–66

Substitute teachers, 93–94. *See also* Floating teachers

Supports

under IDEA, 30

for teachers and administrators, 6

Support staff, 94

Suspension and expulsion policies, 49, 60–61, 63–64, 71–72, 105–106

T

Teaching staff, 90–106
- benefits of working in inclusive settings, 12–13
- child-care teacher's vignette, 99–106
- and developmental assessments, 95–96
- planning time, 97–98
- self-care, 98–99
- support for new teaching styles, 96–97
- teaching assistants, 93–94
- training and professional development, 91–93

Teaching styles, 96–97

Temperature fluctuation, classroom environment, 78

Therapists in the classroom, 65, 94, 102
- benefits of working in inclusive settings, 14–15
- IDEA Part C services, 114
- private therapy practices, 114

Time-outs, 88, 101

Toilet training, vii-viii, 71

Training for teachers, 91–93

Transition to inclusive learning, 52–56
- goal-setting, 53–54
- self-assessment, 52–53
- transition plans, 54–56

Tuition, 59–60
- late payment, 63

U

Universal design for learning (UDL), 6–7

V

Vignettes
- child-care teacher's perspective, 99–106
- director's perspective, 44–51

    parent's perspective, 15–26
    pediatric occupational therapist's perspective, 84–89
Vision statements, 35–37
Visual disabilities/impairment, 44–51, 79
Vocabulary, children's, xi, 89, 105